Why We Cook

WOMEN ON FOOD, IDENTITY, AND CONNECTION

Why We Cook

WOMEN ON FOOD, IDENTITY, AND CONNECTION

LINDSAY GARDNER

WORKMAN PUBLISHING

NEW YORK

Library of Congress Cataloging-in-Publication Data is available.

ISBN 978-1-5235-0974-4

Design by Sarah Smith

The illustrations in this book were made with 140 lb. Arches hot pressed watercolor paper and Holbein Artists' watercolors and gouache.

Workman books are available at special discounts when purchased in bulk for premiums and sales promotions as well as for fundraising or educational use. Special editions or book excerpts can also be created to specification. For details, contact the Special Sales Director at specialmarkets@workman.com.

Workman Publishing Co., Inc.
225 Varick Street
New York, NY 10014-4381

workman.com

Printed in China
First printing January 2021

10 9 8 7 6 5 4 3 2 1

For my mom and my grandmothers,
with infinite gratitude for your
unwavering love, courage, and wisdom,
and for ever emboldening my whys.

+

For Lucy and Maggie.
A stranger once told me that
having two daughters is like having wings.
The two of you are living proof.

Contents

Introduction

WHENEVER I'M OUT with my mom, I know we will always spend a little longer than necessary on everyday interactions. Whether we're on a walk, aboard a plane, or at the hardware store, my mom's curiosity about people and their stories is insatiable. As I was growing up, she was the first person to show me how to look, ask, listen, and pay attention, and that everyone's story matters.

As a wide-eyed kid observing these exchanges, I'm not sure I saw more than friendly small talk. But now, as an adult and a mother myself, I have come to understand that she was teaching me a certain way of walking through the world. And, of course, I find myself doing the same thing, getting caught up in a conversation with the person next to me at the farmers market or at the playground, my own daughters tugging at my shirttails.

Over the years and throughout different phases of my life and career as an artist and illustrator, I've come to realize just how energized I am by these parts of daily life that sometimes slip through our consciousness—moments that seem unremarkable at first glance, but

that hold deeper magic and meaning upon closer examination. I often experience moments like these when I'm cooking, eating, or gathering around the table with my family and friends. Creating something nourishing and beautiful from raw materials that can be shared with others feels like a natural extension of my art practice. The tactile actions and sensations—chopping, whisking, rolling—satisfy my hands; the smells and tastes stimulate my brain; I layer ingredients, colors, and textures on a plate the same way I layer paint on paper. Like art, food can tell a story or ask a question; like art-making, cooking can be a reflection of the concrete and ephemeral, of experience, history, desire, pain, heritage, place, time, emotion, or memory.

One evening in 2018, while cooking dinner for my family, I started wondering why the kitchen draws me back day after day, in much the same way I'm drawn to my art studio. *What is it, exactly, about cooking that makes me feel inspired? Why do I care so much about it, and how does it nourish me in more than the obvious ways? What am I teaching my daughters about the sources, histories, and origins of the food we buy, cook, and put into our bodies, and what will they carry with them as they grow up? What am I teaching them about generosity and self-love? How does this daily ritual on which I expend so much energy relate to my identity as a human, mother, partner, friend, artist, woman?*

I knew I couldn't be the only woman considering these questions (and to be clear, here and in the rest of this book, "woman" refers to anyone who identifies as a woman). A little research led me to a 2018 study that explored trends in home cooking in the United States by gender, education, and race.[1] The study found that from 2003 to 2016, respondents who identified as women spent an average of fifty minutes a day cooking, whereas those who identified as men spent an average of twenty minutes per day. The study also found that 70 percent of women did the cooking in their households, compared to 46 percent of men.

Likewise, women make up a large portion of the professional culinary world. In 2017, the Culinary Institute of America's graduating class was composed of more women than men for the first time in the school's history, and women held 49 percent of entry-level food industry positions.[2] Despite this fact, in 2018, only 23.9 percent of chefs and head cooks were women, and Black, Indigenous, and Women of Color (BIWOC) made up even smaller slices of that percentage.[3] (Across all industries, BIWOC, LGBTQ+ women, and women with disabilities face greater barriers to advancement and face higher rates of workplace discrimination.[4]) With few women and even fewer BIWOC, LGBTQ+ women, and women with disabilities in positions of power, a lack of mentorship, leadership, and management opportunities persists, and the cycle of bias continues. Women often face racism, sexism, and harassment in addition to inequities in industry recognition, media coverage, financial investments, loans, and compensation.[5]

These inequities and aggressions experienced by women have been increasingly documented, particularly since the #MeToo movement began to shake the food world in 2017. Women have begun to speak out more, bravely sharing their experiences and taking action in an effort to create systemic change. And yet, many women's perspectives and achievements continue to be minimized or overlooked; there are many more stories to be heard and much more progress to be made.

Fueled by these facts, my initial questions started to burn even brighter, following me into my studio and paintings and seeping into conversations with friends and family. I started cold calling and interviewing women chefs and food writers, and the circles continued to expand into two years of research. Each conversation flowed into the next; each spurred a new set of questions.

Why We Cook is the result of these conversations—a celebration of women's culinary contributions, achievements, and stories. In this book, you'll find 112 inspiring women who are shaping the contemporary food world as professional chefs, farmers, journalists and authors, food justice activists, restaurateurs, food critics, entrepreneurs, and home cooks (and this list of contributors is by no means static or complete—there are, and will continue to be, so many women doing this work all over the world, every single day). In sharing their stories they expand our collective understanding of the complex, nuanced relationships women have with food and cooking. In essays, interviews, quotes, and recipes, the contributors speak to themes of their choice, including identity, heritage, racial discrimination and intersectionality, resilience and resistance, selfhood, immigration, domesticity, protest, motherhood, memory, family, and relationships, underscoring how food touches every aspect of our lives. Their voices reveal the power of food to sustain, uplift and nourish, channel joy, and effect change, and they offer us all the opportunity to listen. In doing so, we learn about each other, about ourselves, about what we have in common, and also what distinguishes us from one another. There is a place for every woman's story here, including yours.

Since I started working on this project, the world has dramatically changed. As I was submitting my final materials in early 2020, COVID-19 ravaged every corner of the world. It hit the restaurant industry especially hard, triggering closures and precarious working conditions that put workers (especially Black, Indigenous, and People of Color—BIPOC—who make up the majority of essential workers in food and agriculture[6]) at heightened risk of compromised health and unemployment. The virus—and consequential rise in unemployment—also caused an increase in food insecurity due to the disruption of food supply chains and distribution, which in turn exacerbated health inequities, especially among Black and Hispanic families.[7] Simultaneously, the Black Lives Matter movement gained unprecedented and sustained momentum amid the confluence of continual horrific police brutality, the disproportionate impact of COVID-19 on BIPOC, and more than four hundred years of oppression in the United States, forcing all industries—including the food world—to face their complicity in white supremacy and systemic racism.

It is impossible to know where we'll be by the time you are holding this book in your hands. Two things are certain, though: We need real, lasting change, and we need each other more than ever. The stories within these pages offer hope for all that is possible, for learning, empathy, change, equity, and growth, in and out of the kitchen.

These women are writing a new narrative, and it has been a privilege, a joy, and an honor to create art in collaboration with them. Every time I cook, their words and stories are with me, and I am reminded that I am part of a vast web of wisdom larger than any one person, place, or time. Poet Rainer Maria Rilke wrote, "Try to love the *questions themselves* . . . the point is, to live everything. *Live* the questions now." In cooking, my questions begin again and again. And that is why I love it.

My hope is that this book leaves you with more questions than you had when you picked it up. That the next time you go into your kitchen, these women's voices are with you, inspiring you to look deeper. That the next time you cook, gather with loved ones, dine at a restaurant, or chat with a stranger while picking up takeout, you might consider: What can we learn from each other in the kitchen? Why do *you* cook? What are *your* questions, and how can you live them right now?

Ruth Reichl

Ruth Reichl began her legendary career as a food writer in 1972, when she published Mmmmm: A Feastiary, *her first cookbook. The following year, she moved from New York to Berkeley, California, where she lived in a commune, became co-owner and cook at the Swallow restaurant, and contributed to the area's burgeoning culinary revolution.*

In 1978, Reichl became a restaurant critic, writing for New West *and* California *magazines and later for the* Los Angeles Times—*where she was also a food editor—and then the* New York Times. *During her years spent dining in disguise, she became known for her intrepid and equal praise of fine-dining hot spots and little-known restaurants, her wit, her candid exposure of the snobbery and sexism ensconced in the world of haute cuisine, and her sheer delight in the pleasures of eating. In 1999, she left the* New York Times *to become editor in chief of* Gourmet *magazine, where, for a decade, she led the publication to explore the ethics, politics, and stories shaping the food world and to publish approachable recipes, setting a new standard for home cooks before the magazine shuttered in 2009.*

As the author and editor of numerous acclaimed books and anthologies, including five bestselling memoirs, Reichl has been chronicling the evolution of food culture for more than half a century.

Here, Reichl describes a standout meal from each decade of her storied career.

1970–1979

In Berkeley in the seventies, we all believed we could change the world through food. We read *Diet for a Small Planet*, learned that it took twenty pounds of usable protein to make one pound of beef, and became vegetarian. Then we discovered that enormous amounts of food were being thrown away by supermarkets and began dumpster diving. The day I found a perfectly good steak in the dumpster created an ethical dilemma: Should we eat it? Should we let those animals die in vain? After months of millet and rice and beans, we were suddenly omnivores once again. And I have to admit: That steak—cooked with mushrooms foraged up in the hills and served with a salad from our garden and corn we'd grown ourselves—tasted really wonderful.

DUMPSTER DIVE
BERKELEY, CA

1980–1989

Before Blue Hill at Stone Barns in Pocantico Hills, New York, before Blackberry Farm in Walland, Tennessee, there was the New Boonville Hotel. Vernon and Charlene Rollins raised everything they served on the four acres surrounding their Northern California restaurant. Their BLT was the platonic ideal: home-cured bacon, homemade bread, mayonnaise made from their own eggs, and tomatoes still warm from the sun. There were vegetables I'd never tasted before—cardoons, borage, fava beans. It all seemed too good to be true. And it was; their ideas were too big, their resources too small. But thirty years later it turns out they were merely ahead of their time; today, farm-to-table restaurants are all over the country.

NEW BOONVILLE HOTEL
BOONVILLE, CA

1990–1999

I spent a halcyon year writing about the opening of Wolfgang Puck and Barbara Lazaroff's restaurant Chinois on Main, flying back and forth between Berkeley and Santa Monica. Nobody was working on their particular concept of "fusion food," and I was fascinated by the idea of a classically trained European chef honoring his love for Asian food by combining it with European traditions. There were no boundaries; Puck just started playing with ideas. As I wrote in my article for the *Los Angeles Times*, which was published in May 1990, "Opening night was a hectic event: At 6 p.m. the painters were still painting, the electricians were still working, and the cooks were on the verge of hysteria. At 7 there was still chaos. It seemed almost magical, but it all came together, and when the first guests walked in, they entered a serene fantasy of flowers and copper and chinoiserie." And they sat down to eat dishes like sashimi tempura

CHINOIS ON MAIN
LOS ANGELES, CA

and duck, mushrooms and cilantro wrapped in Sichuan pancakes. As for their Chinese chicken salad—which seemed so new to us at the time—it's now served in airports all over the country.

> "The difference between how people thought about food when I first started writing and how people think about food today is very hopeful. We finally understand that food is about much more than deliciousness."

2000–2009

Whenever someone asks "Where should we eat?" my first thought is always Honmura An, the soba restaurant in New York City's SoHo neighborhood. And then I remember that the owner closed the restaurant and went back to Japan after 9/11. But it lingers in my memory as a perfect restaurant, a purely Japanese place with a small, perfectly executed menu. I would begin with cold sake served in a cedar box. A few slices of whatever sashimi owner Koichi Kobari was serving that day. And then the simplest soba, laid out on a bamboo mat with a jar of sauce to dip the strands in. My 1993 review of this restaurant caused an uproar in New York. "She's ruining the standards of the *New York Times*," my predecessor complained, "giving three stars to little Japanese noodle shops." Yup.

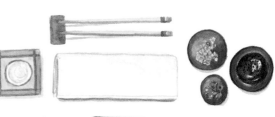

HONMURA AN
NEW YORK, NY

BLUE HILL
NEW YORK, NY

2010–2019

In 2015 Dan Barber, the chef-owner of Blue Hill restaurant in New York, devoted an entire month—in a program he called WastED—to serving nothing but food that would ordinarily have been thrown away. There were the bones of skate, fried to crackling crunchiness and seductively delicious. Salad was made of storage-damaged fruit and vegetables (with a dressing of whipped water from canned beans). Barber conjured vegan burgers out of the pulp left behind at juice bars and made sorbet out of cacao pods. It was dumpster diving on a grand scale—and to someone who started doing that in Berkeley fifty years ago, it was a definite thrill.

Carla Hall

GROWING UP IN Nashville, Tennessee, Carla Hall was always surrounded by soul food but never thought it would become an essential part of her future. After studying business at Howard University in Washington, DC, she worked as an accountant before moving to Paris in her twenties and becoming a runway model. While working, traveling, and eating her way through Europe, Hall began to realize her passion for food. A clarifying moment on her cooking journey, Hall recalls, was during a trip back to the United States to visit friends in Baltimore. She spent days making Julia Child's elaborate recipe for chicken pot pie. Her friends loved it, and she noticed how much satisfaction she derived from bringing joy to others through cooking. Hall decided to move back to DC, where she attended culinary school, started a catering company, and trained in professional restaurant kitchens. In 2008, she launched her television career when she competed on Bravo's *Top Chef* and became known for her optimism and warmth and energetic take on everyday soul food.

Hall's belief in food's power to connect has guided every twist and turn of her career—including overcoming the closure of her Brooklyn-based restaurant, cohosting ABC's *The Chew*, writing award-winning cookbooks, and serving as a culinary ambassador for the Sweet Home Café at the Smithsonian's National Museum of African American History and Culture. "You do something because you want to do it, not because you're expecting a payoff," she says. "And the universe will give it back to you."

"It's not just about breaking bread together, but *making* bread together . . . and telling stories and feeling like we're all in this thing together. That's what I love. Food does that."

Hall travels often, so she revels in time spent at home. "You have to eat, so you may as well try to find the joy in it," she says.

Home Cooks

IN CONVERSATION

WOMEN'S EXPERIENCES COOKING at home are an important, yet often overlooked, part of the modern-day culinary atmosphere and everyday life. No matter how, when, or why we cook, our feelings about food transcend our kitchens and contribute to a complex, diverse, and ever-evolving canon of wisdom.

In this survey, more than 350 women responded to questions about their cooking habits, traditions, and stories, providing insight into how we think about and create meaning through food. Here's an overview of the women who participated in the Home Cooks in Conversation survey.

AGE

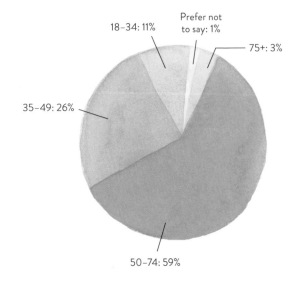

18–34: 11%
Prefer not to say: 1%
75+: 3%
35–49: 26%
50–74: 59%

LOCATION
Within the United States

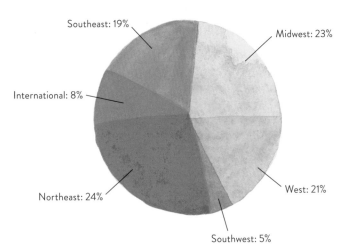

Southeast: 19%
Midwest: 23%
International: 8%
Northeast: 24%
West: 21%
Southwest: 5%

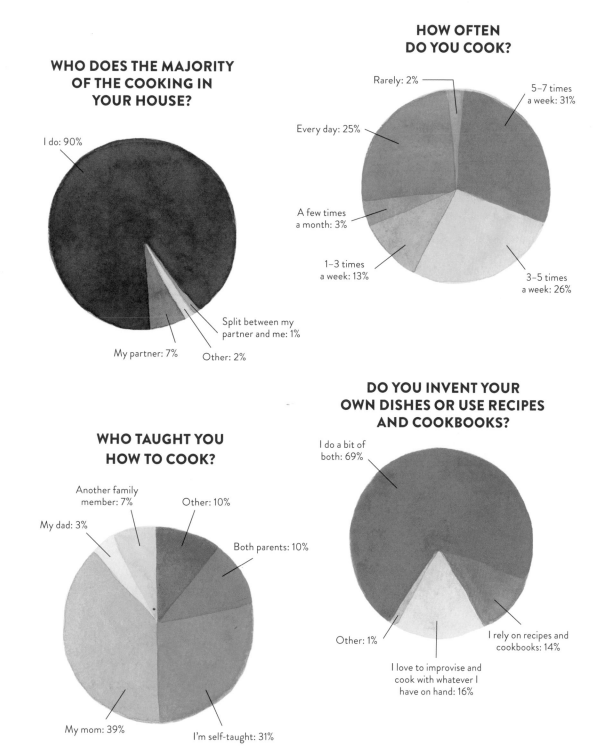

WHO DOES THE MAJORITY OF THE COOKING IN YOUR HOUSE?

I do: 90%

Split between my partner and me: 1%

My partner: 7% Other: 2%

HOW OFTEN DO YOU COOK?

Rarely: 2%

5–7 times a week: 31%

Every day: 25%

A few times a month: 3%

1–3 times a week: 13%

3–5 times a week: 26%

WHO TAUGHT YOU HOW TO COOK?

Another family member: 7%

My dad: 3%

Other: 10%

Both parents: 10%

My mom: 39%

I'm self-taught: 31%

DO YOU INVENT YOUR OWN DISHES OR USE RECIPES AND COOKBOOKS?

I do a bit of both: 69%

Other: 1%

I love to improvise and cook with whatever I have on hand: 16%

I rely on recipes and cookbooks: 14%

Priya Krishna

Priya Krishna is a food writer who contributes regularly to the New York Times, *among other publications. She is also the author of* Indian-ish, *a cookbook that explores her Indian American heritage and celebrates her mother's unique recipes, which were the everyday meals that she grew up with in Dallas, Texas, and are a combination of elements of both cultures. Krishna says her cookbook challenges "a mostly whitewashed interpretation of America and its food." By showing that Indian food is American food, she has carved a much-needed space for the myriad stories, traditions, and innovations that comprise it.*

Kadhi

Serves 4

Meet my favorite soup of all time. Kadhi is similar in texture to cream of _____ soup, but with no cream, and better. All you need to make it are yogurt, chickpea flour, and spices. But don't let the simplicity fool you: Kadhi is both deeply comforting and insanely complex in its flavor, like a cozy blanket draped over a hot bowl of white rice. And my mom's recipe, unlike the liquidy, mild versions I've been served at restaurants, is thick, rich, and spice-forward, with a pleasant tanginess at the end. I absolutely love the strong peppercorn flavor in this dish, but if you don't like peppercorns, feel free to nix them or cut the amount in half.

1 cup full-fat plain yogurt

¼ cup chickpea flour

1 teaspoon ground turmeric

1 tablespoon + 2 tablespoons ghee or olive oil, divided

½ teaspoon + 1 teaspoon cumin seeds, divided

½ teaspoon black mustard seeds

½ teaspoon fenugreek seeds

5 whole cloves

2 bay leaves

½ teaspoon whole black peppercorns

1 teaspoon kosher salt, plus more if needed

Lime juice (optional, if your yogurt is not that sour)

¼ teaspoon red chile powder

3 dried red chiles

½ teaspoon asafetida (optional, but really great)

1 In a large (at least 2-cup) measuring cup with a spout (for easy pouring), mix together the yogurt and chickpea flour until smooth and homogeneous. Stir in 1 cup water, followed by the turmeric—the mixture should be a pale yellow color. Set aside.

2 In a very large, deep pot or Dutch oven over medium heat, warm 1 tablespoon of the ghee (or oil). Once the ghee melts (or the oil begins to shimmer), add ½ teaspoon of the cumin seeds, the black mustard seeds, fenugreek, cloves, bay leaves, and peppercorns all at once and cook until you hear the mustard seeds start to pop, 1 to 2 minutes. Reduce the heat to low, add the yogurt–chickpea flour mixture and 3 cups water, and mix well. Add the salt. Taste—the mixture should be tangy, rich, and distinctly flavored by the spices. Adjust with a few drops of lime juice and more salt if needed. Increase the heat to high and cook, stirring continuously (if you stop stirring, the kadhi will curdle), until the mixture comes to a boil. Insert a large long-handled spoon into the pot to prevent it from boiling over and let cook on high for 10 minutes (if at any point it looks like it might boil over, reduce the heat to medium-high for a minute before turning it back up). The kadhi should become thicker and brighter in color, like a creamy soup.

❸ About 5 minutes before the kadhi is done cooking, in a small pan or butter warmer over medium-high heat, warm the remaining 2 tablespoons ghee (or oil). Once the ghee melts (or the oil begins to shimmer), add the remaining 1 teaspoon cumin seeds and cook until it starts to sputter and turn brown, which should take seconds. Immediately remove the pan from the heat and stir in the chile powder, dried chiles, and asafetida (if using).

❹ Add the seasoning to the cooked kadhi and stir to combine.

❺ Serve with rice.

"I have learned to embrace both sides of my heritage. I used to feel too American to be considered Indian, and too Indian to be considered American. Those identities, I've realized, don't have to be compartmentalized."

ESSAY BY

Gray Chapman

Gray Chapman is an Atlanta-based journalist who writes about food, spirits, and culture. Her work has appeared in the New York Times, Atlanta *magazine,* Garden & Gun, Punch, *and other publications.*

Cookbook Club

A short list of things I've learned in the year since I began participating in an all-women's cookbook club:

- Every bottle of sherry vinegar in the metro Atlanta area will seemingly vanish from shelves the day you need to make David Chang's pickled mushrooms.

- Driving with a Dutch oven full of beans riding shotgun will almost certainly result in hot bean water sloshing on your passenger seat.

- Tossing thirty dried chile peppers into a ripping hot skillet will inevitably hotbox the entire kitchen with capsaicin fumes, resulting in a dozen women fleeing to the back porch, clutching their throats, gasping for air, and laughing hysterically.

Another thing I've learned is that laboring over something beautiful, simply for the sake of sharing it with others, is a rarified thing of beauty in and of itself.

When my neighbor Sue first floated the idea of a cookbook club—a group of her friends from different circles who mostly didn't know one another, all with varying levels of culinary experience, all united by a love for cooking—I was, frankly, intimidated. Intimidated by the

idea of cooking for an unfamiliar crowd. Intimidated by the recipes and the prospect of sourcing ingredients, especially for our first pick (a double whammy of Yotam Ottolenghi's *Jerusalem* and *NOPI*). Intimidated by other women, period.

At home, cooking is a hobby, but it's also my self-soothing mechanism for days when I'm gripped by anxiety about my work, my future, the world. That is to say, I cook nearly every day. But I'm not an entertainer. I don't do dinner parties. I lack my mother's gilded hostess skills. I get a tingle of performance anxiety when other people watch me dice an onion.

Most of the time, I'm only cooking for myself and my husband. We have an equitable marriage, and we relentlessly support one another in our creative work, but our kitchen seems to function as a time machine, transporting part of our marriage back to the 1950s. I am "the one who cooks," which means that, usually, I am also the one who plans meals, keeps a continuous mental tally of our fridge's inventory, and, when texted at 4:30 p.m. "What should we do for dinner tonight?" is expected

to have an answer and a plan. When someone else cooks for me, it is often either because I am paying them to, or because she is my mother.

Yet it was for Cookbook Club that I found myself gridlocked in Atlanta traffic for an hour on a quest for cascabel chiles to make Gabriela Cámara's puerco al pastor. Because for just one night every other month, the notion of practicality flies out the window. On those nights, and the frenetic day or two leading up to them, "dinner" is no longer simply an answer to that 4:30 p.m. text. It's one night in which easy sheet pan meals and Instant Pot hacks take a backseat to care, time, and attention, not because we have to, but because we want to. It's why, for the same dinner, I ignored the generic black beans in my cabinet and drove across town to buy two pounds of Rancho Gordo's Ayocote Negro heirlooms. And it's why, later that night, a few of us stood shoulder to shoulder in the kitchen hunched over masa, press, and skillet, making tortillas one by one.

It is all effort, but one that is never not reciprocated or shared. No one ever articulated that homemade tortillas would be mandatory, or that finding cascabels would be required. But I suspect it happens anyway because it feels like a rare chance to slow down, both for and alongside each other, to appreciate the process as much as the end result.

For us, the nature of gathering like this means squeezing in our ingredient quests after work, delegating childcare, dipping out of work events early, staying up late the night before to prep. Real life makes it difficult to source that AWOL vinegar or that one special ingredient that you could probably fudge, if you really wanted to. I find that none of us ever do.

That first night, it was all anyone could talk about: *How could all of this possibly taste so good?* We looked around and sat in awe of what we had made. The recipes themselves were exceptional, of course. Still, there was something else. "It's home-cooked," one of the women finally said.

To feed one another, and to be fed—that felt as revelatory as the piles of truffle-tossed baby carrots, steaming mejadra, and saffron rice sitting before us. We picked up our forks and began to eat.

Julia Turshen

In addition to being a cook, food writer, and bestselling cookbook author, Julia Turshen is a passionate advocate for civil rights and social justice.

One of the most important meals I've ever had lasted for nearly twenty-four hours. It was during the summer of 2017 and took place at my kitchen table. I invited a group of friends who all work in and around food. Our group had been in touch here and there before the meal, and we were all craving some in-person time to sit and reflect and connect on the things we had been talking about over group texts. Top of our list was the lack of racial diversity in food media.

Once everyone arrived at my house (a couple of hours north of New York City), we never left the kitchen table except to sleep. We just kept talking and eating. Talking and eating. We kept refilling the table with fruit and cheese and chocolate and other snacks and eventually cleared it for a lamb stew that I had made the day before. I spent most of the time listening.

Hearing from friends about their experiences has helped inform so many decisions I make and actions I take in my work. About a year after that meal, I founded Equity at the Table, an inclusive digital directory of women and nonbinary individuals in food. And the people who sat around my kitchen table that summer are now on the advisory board.

Leah Penniman

LEAH PENNIMAN IS a Black Kreyol educator, farmer, author, and food justice activist. In 2011, she cofounded Soul Fire Farm, a Black-, Indigenous-, and People of Color (BIPOC)–centered farm in Grafton, New York, that is dedicated to ending racism in the food system. As co-executive director, Penniman facilitates the farm's food sovereignty programs, including farmer training for BIPOC and subsidized food distribution for communities in need; teaches Indigenous and regenerative farming practices; and oversees workshops, youth programs, and special events.

Penniman's work instills a sense of possibility and connection to the land and educates BIPOC on the relationships between the earth and history, socioeconomics, politics, and philosophy. "Everything from sunshine to plate needs to be infused with fairness and dignity and reverence,"

she says. "That means that the land is shared and the earth is regarded with respect, that farm workers are treated with dignity and paid fairly, and that everyone gets enough culturally appropriate life-giving food to eat."

A Day at Soul Fire Farm

Here, Penniman gives a snapshot of her life on the farm during the summer of 2019.

There's rarely a typical day. I usually wake up around 5:30 or 6 a.m. and sneak in a run. Then I facilitate a meeting for the visiting teachers who are helping with our weeklong immersion program—BIPOC FIRE (Black–Indigenous–People of Color Farming in Relationship with Earth)—for people who want to learn basic skills in Afro-Indigenous and regenerative farming. Then I go outside to lead a stretch for the twenty program participants who gathered here from all around the country.

In my first work block, I harvest cherries, blueberries, and currants with my group and then do a little bit of mulching around those plants. Other groups follow different farmers to do tasks like taking care of the chickens or planting seeds in the greenhouse.

At breakfast, everyone shares a highlight, an opportunity, and a challenge. Then we go over the schedule for the day with our participants and head back out to the farm for the long work block. Today I am teaching a group how to dig a new raised bed in the style of the Ovambo people of Angola and Namibia, and then we will plant the bed with the three sisters (corn, beans, and squash), the way the Mohican farmers taught us.

Midday, we do an around-the-world exercise where folks teach each other what they've learned in their work blocks. There is also a variety of workshops going on, and I might run inside to do some administrative work and give input on the Green New Deal.

In the afternoon, I teach classes. I have a soil science class, an agroforestry class, and a class on the history of Black Indigenous farming movements. Black folks and Indigenous folks have a ten-thousand-plus-year history of dignity and innovation on the land. Knowing that the Egyptians during Cleopatra's reign were some of the first people to come up with worm composting, that the folks in Kenya were among the first to come up with terraces, that Dr. George Washington Carver brought regenerative agriculture to the mainstream in the United States, and so forth is crucial in reclaiming our dignity and belonging in this story.

Before dinner, I'll sneak in a bit more administrative work to plan upcoming workshops and travel. At dinner, we break out into tables by home regions to talk about current and potential projects. Afterward, there's an action-planning workshop that I help with. So, it's about a 6 a.m. to 10 p.m. day most of the time in the summer.

BELOW
Soul Fire Farm's main house and gathering center, which were built by hand using local timber and are heated with solar energy

"When young people see Black and Brown folks running a farm, building their own house, running their own business, they say, 'Well, if your dreams can come true, maybe mine can too.'"

"For me food is a prayer and a protest. It is a sacred practice inherited from all my relations. The stories of food inspire empathy and connection. Food is about relationships and survival and creating the future."

—Jocelyn Jackson

cook activist, founder of JUSTUS Kitchen, and cofounder of People's Kitchen Collective

In what area are you most passionate about impacting change?

"Politics and local government. I'm building upon my background as a food justice activist within local politics and advocating for programs and policies that promote a more fair and inclusive San Francisco. I'm also passionate about getting more young people, women, queer folks, and people of color to be engaged in and lead our civic and political processes."

—Shakirah Simley
director of the Office of Racial Equity for
the City and County of San Francisco
and founder of Nourish | Resist
San Francisco, CA

"We usually only hear about food from a chef's or owner's perspective. You have to treat everyone fairly and include everybody in these conversations."

—Martha Hoover
restaurateur and founder of
Patachou Inc. and the Patachou Foundation
Indianapolis, IN

"Amplifying new voices and impactful ideas through connection and collaboration. I try to really understand what people are aiming for and the changes they're working toward. Then I work to share their stories with new communities. I'm able to do this through the programs I write because food is such a powerful connector."

—Maryam Ahmed
consultant, coach, and creator of
the Diversity in Wine Leadership Forum
Napa, CA

"Food is a universal need, and learning to cook for oneself is a life skill. Disabled people not being represented in the culinary community and having neither sufficient role models nor adaptive inspiration means there is a need going unmet.

"Drawing from my own experience with a disability, I created *The Fingerless Kitchen*, a cooking show that inspires and teaches people with disabilities how to cook and helps them see that their limitations are opportunities to do something different and amazing. I want everyone to remember that if you think you're all thumbs in the kitchen, I'm here to prove that you never needed them."

—Bryony Grealish
founder and owner of the Fingerless Kitchen
Syracuse, NY

What is your wish for the future?

"The world is so complicated. I wish there was no suffering, particularly due to the lack of food access. The food distribution systems are politically charged and flawed. Knowing that there are children in my city, children within a mile of my restaurant locations, who don't know what they're going to eat at home tonight bothers me significantly. And knowing that there are people around the world who are unable to access food at all—it's just gut-wrenching."

—Martha Hoover
restaurateur and founder of
Patachou Inc. and the Patachou Foundation
Indianapolis, IN

"That the culinary industry starts to effect measurable change on social issues. Not just waiting for new policies, but revolutionizing the way we've always done it. Some are already doing this, but we need more. Food is power."

—Maryam Ahmed
consultant, coach, and creator of
the Diversity in Wine Leadership Forum
Napa, CA

"I want to see more green in our hoods, I want to see more accessibility to knowledge of plant-based foods and options for the community, I want to see capitalist fast-food corporations shut down and our people rise up. I want there to be a food revolution— people planting together, interacting with one another, trading produce, talking to their kids about the benefits of a plant-based lifestyle. I want to see a world where people will make a change, however they can and have the ability to, for our earth, their communities, and themselves."

—Amy Quichiz
founder of Veggie Mijas, writer, and activist
New York, NY

"For people with disabilities to be proportionately represented and integrated throughout the food industry and to make the stigma and discrimination directed at people with disabilities a thing of the past. More adaptive technologies, more visibility through cooking shows and publications, more access to jobs, and an overall feeling of personal accomplishment, enjoyment, and connection in the kitchen."

—Bryony Grealish
founder and owner of the Fingerless Kitchen
Syracuse, NY

Abra Berens

ABRA BERENS IS like a kid in a candy store, except her candy store is Granor Farm in southwest Michigan, where, as the head chef, she is immersed in a bounty of freshly harvested vegetables. She firmly believes that "the meals we eat should change with the seasons, and their ingredients should come from nearby," a philosophy she's honed over a decade of experience as a farmer and chef. At Granor Farm, Berens channels her passion into creating unique dinners with the produce grown just steps from the farmhouse door. These communal meals (served in the farmhouse) reinforce the direct connection between the farm and diners' plates, celebrating the diverse agriculture of the region and giving guests a behind-the-scenes look at organic farming.

BELOW

Granor Farm in Three Oaks, Michigan, where Chef Berens hosts weekly dinners in the farmhouse

Buttermilk and Butter Lettuce Salad

Serves 4 to 6 as a side

I've never been much of a butter lettuce person, always finding it pleasant enough but not especially exciting on the palate. That is, until I started eating the butter lettuce we grow at Granor Farm. Good butter lettuce has large, delicate leaves and a deep, grassy flavor that's usually found in darker greens. This salad came from my desire to showcase those leaves by serving them whole and not drowning them in dressing. By fanning all the ingredients out horizontally and dressing them in layers, the flavor of the leaves shines through with support from the stronger flavors of buttermilk and tomatoes. Plus, any time I can dress a vegetable with something as often overlooked as straight buttermilk, it feels like a victory!

¼ cup olive oil, plus more for pan-roasting tomatoes

1 pound cherry tomatoes

2 cloves garlic, peeled and minced

Zest and juice of 1 lemon

1 bunch flat-leaf (Italian) parsley, chopped

½ teaspoon salt, plus extra for seasoning

1 head butter lettuce, leaves separated, washed, and dried

Freshly ground black pepper, for seasoning

½ cup buttermilk

¼ cup sunflower seeds, toasted

❶ In a medium-size frying pan, warm a glug of olive oil and pan-roast the tomatoes over medium-high heat until they burst and their liquid reduces, stirring occasionally, 10 to 15 minutes. When the tomatoes are roasted, allow them to cool.

❷ Combine ¼ cup olive oil with the garlic, lemon zest and juice, parsley, and salt in a small bowl to make a chunky relish.

❸ When ready to serve, lay out half the butter lettuce leaves on a large serving platter and sprinkle with salt and pepper. Spoon half the tomatoes evenly over the lettuce, followed by half the garlic relish and half the buttermilk. Repeat with the remaining ingredients and top with the sunflower seeds before serving.

What is your favorite part of the cooking process?

"My favorite part of the cooking process is sharing it with my peers. Their being a part of the process and learning along the way is most gratifying to me."

—Mimi Mendoza
pastry chef at Senia
Honolulu, HI

"I think the cooking process in a restaurant is different than at home. Having the freedom to experiment at home is really fun, and that improvisation can lead to some really great ideas. In the restaurant kitchen, seeing a dish come together on the line, sometimes with the contribution of a few different stations, is really satisfying. It's like seeing the solution of a puzzle play out repeatedly!"

—Cheetie Kumar
chef and owner of Garland, Neptunes Parlour,
and Kings and rock guitarist
Raleigh, NC

"While I love all the steps and find the entire cooking process therapeutic, seeing someone eat the food is definitely my favorite part. The first cooking lessons I learned from my mother were to always cook with love and that your emotions affect the taste of the food. Seeing someone happily eating something you've made is the transference of your own energy. It causes the person to feel something, and that is why I love feeding people— they get vulnerable and let themselves release a little of the control they have to always have in place in order to exist in the world."

—Rose Previte
restaurateur and owner of
Maydān and Compass Rose
Washington, DC

"I love the experimentation and the prep—playing with spices and different techniques and hitting on something through that process. I am my most creative during the process as opposed to sitting in front of a blank piece of paper or plate."

—Preeti Mistry
chef, entrepreneur, speaker, and activist
Oakland, CA

"I love that when we bake, we transform the simplest ingredients into things that can bring great pleasure to the people we love. After all these years, I still think that baking is magic."

—**Dorie Greenspan**
writer, *New York Times Magazine* columnist, and author
New York, NY, and Paris, France

"I have two favorite parts of the cooking process. The first is ideation: When I am thinking about a dish, it is almost like I am sketching it in my mind. Adding, taking away, erasing, adjusting, moving components. . . . That time when you are not sure what it will become is very special and exciting.

"My second favorite part is seeing someone eat the food. At my core, I am a feeder. I love how universal yet individual the act of enjoying food can be. Some people like to eat quickly and aggressively. Others would rather savor every morsel. Some people like to be stimulated and made to think while eating. Others prefer it to be a simple and basic experience. I truly enjoy being a part of anyone's experience."

—**Katianna Hong**
chef
Los Angeles, CA

"My favorite part is the procurement and getting to know the people behind the ingredients: the farmers, foragers, fishermen. You have so much more respect for the food when you know where your money goes and how those families use those funds."

—**Kristen Essig**
co-chef and co-owner of Coquette and Thalia
New Orleans, LA

Ana Roš

WHEN ANA ROŠ took over operations at Hiša Franko in Kobarid, Slovenia, with her life and business partner, Valter Kramar, in 2000, she had no culinary training. Since then, the entirely self-taught chef has been credited with putting Slovenian gastronomy on the map. In 2019, Hiša Franko appeared on the World's 50 Best Restaurants list for the second year in a row, and in 2020, the restaurant was awarded two Michelin stars.

Kobarid, home to about one thousand people, is located in Slovenia's rugged alpine Soča Valley, along Italy's northeast border. Here, Hiša Franko has become the hub

of an intricate network of farmers, foragers, vintners, shepherds, fishermen, and cheesemakers, all of whom supply the restaurant with hyperlocal ingredients: a "win-win situation," as Roš calls it.

She relies on in-house and local foragers to bring her the delicate, wild plants she prizes: ramson, purslane, and black trumpet mushrooms, to name a few. Neighboring farmers often bring her an excess of their harvest; she buys it anyway and finds a way to use it. Working with a nearby fishery research institute, Roš was one of the first chefs in the region to experiment with cooking and eating

RIGHT

Black marble trout immersed in a verdant broth that evokes a riverbed

BELOW

Roš's life, work, and community are intimately tied to the four seasons: pomlad, poletje, jesen, and zima (spring, summer, autumn, winter).

POMLAD

POLETJE

> "We are always aware of our environment, of the season, of the territory. Every single dish has a characteristic of foraging because we are trying to connect it to the environment where we work."

black marble trout as a way to help repopulate the once-endangered native species. These practices and relationships are cultivated as much for sourcing ingredients as they are to ensure mutual survival—the restaurant's, the community's, and the larger ecosystem's—and Roš is equally passionate about both.

Her approach is akin to that of an artist or scientist: She's motivated by fierce curiosity and an unrelenting desire to learn, innovate, and evolve. As a result, Roš's cuisine is both a reflection of the Soča Valley's regional specialties and a window into her independent spirit, evident in her artful manipulation of ingredients born from the mountains, forests, and rivers of the wild and ever-changing countryside.

JESEN

ZIMA

Renee Erickson

A SEATTLE NATIVE, chef Renee Erickson grew up fishing and crabbing with her father in Puget Sound and is now a fervent advocate for protecting the area's waterways and sea life. After graduating from college with a fine arts degree, she traveled through Europe, where she fell in love with French cuisine. When she returned to Seattle, she apprenticed with Boat Street Café's chef and owner, Susan Kaplan, before eventually buying the restaurant in 1998. Erickson's work there set the stage for future projects, cementing her passion for French cooking and her zeal for highlighting the abundance of local produce and seafood in the Pacific Northwest.

She later cofounded Seattle's Sea Creatures—a bustling restaurant group that now consists of ten eateries, including the Whale Wins and the Walrus and the Carpenter (which Erickson has described as "a Pacific Northwest fish shack meets Parisian oyster bar"). Erickson chose to supply all of Sea Creatures's restaurants with sustainably caught seafood from local, environmentally friendly fisheries, and in 2018, she removed Chinook salmon, a crucial source of nutrition for migrating orca whales in the Pacific Ocean, from her menus.

Erickson has also worked with the Environmental Defense Fund to bring attention to the dangers of overfishing and the decline of ocean fish populations, and she is involved in grassroots efforts to protect

LEFT

Erickson trimming asparagus from her backyard garden in Seattle. Her kitchen is adorned with vintage dishes and antique knives that she collected on trips to France over the years, an echo of the eclectic aesthetic in all of her restaurants.

salmon watersheds throughout the Pacific Northwest from potentially catastrophic drilling and mining. "I love the relationships you get to have in this business, with farmers, fishermen, cheesemakers, all the artists making beautiful things. . . .

All of it is so important—hearing their stories and hardships, then teaching your teams to appreciate it all and understand why it's worth caring for these ingredients and creating beautiful food," says Erickson.

"One of the greatest things I've learned from cooking is that food is more about the context in which it is created than how it is cooked. Even the most methodical, mundane aspects of cooking become magical when you know why and for whom you are creating food."

—Reem Assil

chef and owner of Reem's California, entrepreneur, and activist

Yewande Komolafe

WRITER, RECIPE DEVELOPER, and food stylist Yewande Komolafe is originally from Lagos, Nigeria. She moved to the United States when she was sixteen to attend college, but due to an administrative error made by the university, she lost her student visa and became undocumented.

During the twenty years when Komolafe could not return to Nigeria, food provided a crucial link to her home country and family. After graduating from culinary school, she worked in prestigious restaurant and test kitchens, but because of her undocumented status, she kept her Nigerian cooking to herself—it was a private pastime that helped her feel closer to her parents and childhood identity.

Today, Komolafe lives in Brooklyn with her husband and daughter and operates her recipe development lab, Four Salt Spoons, where she creates recipes for cookbooks, magazines, and other publications, including *Saveur*, *Bon Appétit*, and the *New York Times*. Her cooking—informed by her travels, by her grandmothers', mother's, and aunts' cooking, and by memories of the food she ate as a child—has become a way for her to navigate calling two countries home.

When Donald Trump's 2016 presidential race increased anti-immigration rhetoric, Komolafe felt compelled to speak out about her nationality and immigration status. She created My Immigrant Food Is . . . , a monthly dinner series she hosts in Brooklyn, often in collaboration with other immigrants and culinarians. At each dinner, Komolafe serves locally sourced Nigerian fare for thirty to forty guests, who gather around the table, sharing stories and building community.

On page 37, Komolafe shares the story of her first meal at her family's house after two decades.

My flight to Lagos arrives at dusk, and I slide into an airport humming with the activity of nocturnal commerce and community. For me, it's a confusion of crowds after the stillness of a thirteen-hour flight. My parents drive my husband and me to their house, and we see shadows along the roadside, forms emerging from the headlights' edges and plunging back into the darkness. Lagos is a city by the sea. Its streets are never silent, never still. A quick glance and all seems calm. But if you look closely, people are filling up the dark, like a tide rolling in and receding. They're striding, chatting in groups, gathering by a food stand on the edge of a streetlight's glow. They are carrying into the middle of the night a city bursting with energy and life.

As we drive up Adeniyi Jones Road to the gated community where my parents live, my mother points out landmarks from my childhood. None are immediately recognizable, but her voice is all the familiarity I need: I'm strangely, and impossibly, home. I breathe in the air and feel every inch of my person expand. We step out of the car, and the heat, the gorgeous glow of old incandescent bulbs in faded sconces, and the foliage fill every inch of our yard. Lemongrass, wild oregano, and scent leaf suffuse the air as I walk up to the front door.

My parents' home in Ikeja, Lagos, is concrete and glass amid a green oasis. From the dining room I can make out the shape of a banana tree in the corner of the garden. Bright yellow starfruit hang low on another. Everything is ripe and ready for picking. I hear chickens clucking, settling in for the night.

Dinner is a light meal of stewed chicken and greens in obe ata (a fiery sauce of tomatoes, red bell peppers, and chiles), with fried sweet plantains and steamed rice. The scent leaf I noticed in the garden has been julienned, garnishing the dishes. It is my first time back in my parents' kitchen in twenty years. On the plate before me, all the complexities of a life lived in exile intermingle with the simplicity of home.

How do you overcome creative ruts?

"Go out to a really nice dinner. Read. Travel."

—Anita Lo
chef, culinary tour guide, and author
New York, NY

"I look at the work of others through cookbooks, dining, and travel. I'm inspired by all the different flavors that can be achieved depending on the combination of ingredients."

—Tanya Holland
chef and owner of Brown Sugar Kitchen,
television personality, and speaker
Oakland, CA

"I always go to the farmers market once a week, sometimes twice. Usually, ingredients that are in season at the same time go together perfectly. Nature makes the most balanced dishes, and I just try to get out of its way."

—Caroline Glover
chef and founder of Annette
Aurora, CO

"When I find myself in a creative rut, I like to travel. My husband and I like to go somewhere new abroad at least once a year. Experiencing other cultures and their food and traditions really helps us grow as chefs. We always come back rejuvenated and inspired.

"As chefs, we often forget to pause and engage in something other than our work. When I force myself to pause, I become inspired by unsuspecting things: eating a casual meal out, visiting a museum, reading a book, going to a park. Slowing down to speed up."

—Katianna Hong
chef
Los Angeles, CA

"I visit artists, whether in the form of museums or galleries, their Instagram pages, or large-format books. I find art to be extremely inspiring, from the content to the colors."

—Kristen Essig
co-chef and co-owner of Coquette and Thalia
New Orleans, LA

Celia Sack

CELIA SACK HAS been a treasure hunter for as long as she can remember. "Book scouting is my favorite thing in the world," she says. "It's the highest I get!"

For almost a decade, Sack worked as a modern literature and rare books specialist at Pacific Book Auction in Berkeley, California, where she honed her love of culinary books and food history and grew her private antiquarian cookbook collection. In 2008, she opened her inviting, jewel box–like bookshop, Omnivore Books in San Francisco, to share her passion with like-minded people and "geek out all day." In the shop, Sack buys and sells new, vintage, and collectible books on food and drink and hosts popular events.

Sack sees cookbooks as an especially important form of storytelling. "They tell so much about what was going on at the time, and not just in a social way, but also with the foods that were available and the way things were cooked," she says. Equally compelling is the physical evidence of well-traversed pages: intimate and touching inscriptions; notes and stains; soft, worn spines.

The depth of Sack's knowledge and her ability to recall titles, editions, publication dates, and historical context are nothing short of astounding. She is as excited to pore over obscure gems like a nineteenth-century ice cream manual or a copy of *The History of the Use of Ostrich Eggs over Time* as she is to discuss the poetic recipes of Judy Rodgers's *The Zuni Cafe Cookbook* (her personal favorite) with a customer. Her generous spirit, coupled with her expertise and knack for unearthing treasures, have made Omnivore Books a destination, where she has befriended and

hosted cookbook authors and editors, food writers, chefs, and home cooks alike.

This ever-expanding constellation is Sack's pride and joy: She has transported out-of-print books on Danish agriculture to Noma's René Redzepi; introduced Alice Waters to volumes on World War I–era victory gardens; and helped Ruth Reichl find a rare edition of her favorite book on 1940s Parisian cuisine. Like a stealthy time traveler, Sack weaves a web across place and time, culture and information, connecting people with histories, stories, science, curiosities, and wisdom they may not have even known they needed. But for her, it's quite simple: "I love the trail that these books take. And I love thinking about where they've been," she reflects. "That is just so fun for me—to know that the book is going to the right place, exactly the right place."

Nicole Ponseca

NICOLE PONSECA WAS born to Filipino immigrants in Philadelphia, and raised in a predominantly white suburb of San Diego, California. She grew up eating the food of her parents' home country, but when she moved to New York to pursue a job in advertising, she was surprised at the lack of Filipino food in Manhattan and the corresponding lack of media attention to Filipino cuisine. Eager to learn all she could about the food industry, she worked in restaurants in her spare time and eventually quit her day job to pursue a career as a restaurateur.

Ponseca channeled her passion for her Filipino heritage and the country's multifaceted cuisine into cofounding two New York City restaurants, Maharlika in 2011 and Jeepney in 2015, with executive chef Miguel Trinidad. Ponseca is often credited with introducing authentic Filipino food and staples of the cuisine—pig's ears and snout, balut (fertilized duck egg), ube (purple yam), chicken feet, and salted egg—largely unfamiliar to an American audience.

Bibingka

Serves 4 to 6

I didn't grow up eating bibingka, but if I had the chance to do it all over again, I'd gladly switch out all the cinnamon buns for this easy-to-make skillet snack. It's everything one could want in a snack—it's a lil' bit sweet, a wee bit savory, and uniquely Filipino. Just like me. Now, I've had this dish in America, but let's be honest, it's never gonna be exactly like it is back in the motherland, where it's made with fresh carabao's milk cheese, cooked over charcoal, and enjoyed roadside at the churches that make it Sundays after service in the town of Laguna. I hope you make this. I hope you sink your teeth into it. And I hope you think of me. xoxo.

1 Preheat the oven to 350°F. Grease a 9-inch cast-iron skillet or baking dish with butter or cooking spray and line it with the banana leaf. Trim the edges of the leaf so that it hangs over the skillet or dish by only an inch or 2, then coat the leaf with more butter or spray.

2 In a large bowl, stir together the rice flour, sugar, baking powder, and salt.

3 In a medium-size bowl, beat together the coconut milk, whole milk, melted butter, and raw eggs until well combined.

4 Slowly mix the wet ingredients into the dry ingredients, making sure they are well incorporated.

5 Pour the batter into the prepared skillet or baking dish and top it with the salted egg slices.

6 Bake for 20 minutes, or until a toothpick inserted into the center comes out clean. Brush the top with the condensed milk and sprinkle with the cheese. Return the pan to the oven and bake just until the cheese melts, 1 to 2 minutes more.

7 Let cool slightly, then cut into slices and serve still warm or at room temperature.

Butter or cooking spray, for greasing

1 banana leaf, washed and dried

1 cup glutinous rice flour

1 cup sugar

2½ teaspoons baking powder

⅛ teaspoon kosher salt

1 cup coconut milk

¼ cup whole milk

3 tablespoons unsalted butter, melted

3 large eggs

1 salted egg or hard-boiled egg, peeled and sliced

3 tablespoons condensed milk

½ cup grated Edam cheese

Recipe adapted from *I Am a Filipino* by Nicole Ponseca and Miguel Trinidad. Copyright © 2018 by Nicole Ponseca and Miguel Trinidad. Used by permission of Artisan, a division of Workman Publishing Co., Inc., New York. All rights reserved.

Dorie Greenspan

DORIE GREENSPAN IS a cookbook author and *New York Times Magazine* columnist whose work has earned the respect and adoration of professional chefs and home cooks alike. After accidentally burning down her parents' Brooklyn kitchen at age twelve, she did not cook again until she became a parent. She immersed herself in cooking, baking, and, later, writing about food, expanding her affinity for French cooking and baking and even scoring an apprenticeship with Julia Child.

Now she splits her time among New York, Paris, and Connecticut, all of which she considers home. "I've always considered myself lucky that I've had the chance to do the work that I do—it wasn't what I expected to do in my life and I came to it late—and so I'm grateful to be able to continue doing it and to know that it makes others happy," she reflects.

"My Paris kitchen is cramped but efficient, filled with light, has double doors out to a balcony, and seems to work well when I'm cooking for two and when we're eight for dinner."

"I've lived and worked in our New York apartment for decades. I learned to cook and bake in that kitchen, and I became a writer there too. This is where I would bake with our son, and where the two of us would sit on the counters and talk over things that were important then and still seem important now. It's as though the kitchen and I are partners—we've been together so long that we know each other's moves."

LEFT
Greenspan's Paris kitchen

BELOW
Greenspan baking in her New York City kitchen

Abby Fuller

Abby Fuller's fascination with storytelling took root at a young age. She recalls constantly penning stories and making short films with her parents' video camera during her childhood in upstate New York. Now the first woman director for the Netflix documentary series Chef's Table, *Fuller shares the stories and voices of women and people of color in food (her episodes featuring Mashama Bailey and Cristina Martinez— see page 72—are regarded as some of the series' most lauded).*

In 2015, her first assignment for Chef's Table *took her to rural Slovenia to document the life and work of chef Ana Roš (see page 30). The three weeks she spent there, chronicling Roš's passion for seasonality and innovation, inspired Fuller to seek a deeper understanding of ecology and her own relationship to the natural world.*

Shortly after Fuller returned to the United States, she moved from California to rural Virginia, where she joined her now-husband on Another Perfect Day (APD), a farm that uses regenerative grazing practices to raise high-quality, grass-fed cattle for butcheries and restaurants, conduct soil research, and heal degraded ecosystems.

Today, Fuller's multifaceted creative ambitions are inseparable from her deep connection to the land and its seasonal cycles, whether she's researching a story, filming on location for Chef's Table *or another documentary project (her latest film,* Shepherd's Song, *tells the story of a nomadic shepherdess preventing wildfires across Central California's grasslands), cooking, or gardening at the farm.*

A Year at Another Perfect Day Farm

Spring

During the long months and short days of winter, when the land is covered in tawny brown vegetation, I sometimes lose hope that spring will ever come. But it does. And when it arrives, there is a seismic shift in energy. Extended hours of sunshine are felt by everything around us. Southern magnolia trees come to life and bloom giant ivory flowers.

The pasture becomes thick and green and fills with dozens of grasses, legumes, and herbs. Bees collect nectar, butterflies float among the pasture, and barn swallows dance through the sky chasing flies. Spring is also calving season: Mama cows give birth daily, and every day I have the opportunity to witness the calves' first steps.

Summer

When summer hits, the days are long, hot, and humid. The rhythmic hum of cicadas fills the air, and we spend evenings quietly tending the garden. After much preparation, vegetables begin steadily producing, often yielding overwhelming surpluses of tomatoes, cucumbers, and giant zucchinis. There is intimacy in eating this way. We give the garden what it needs in the spring in the form of rotting hay, manure, old straw, compost, and fish emulsion, and then the garden gives its bounty to us in the summer.

Fall

Fall is the season of red and orange woodland edges as the sour gum and maple trees begin to turn. Wild persimmons and pawpaws begin ripening. We also harvest Georgia Candy Roasters from the garden, a rare squash originally bred by the Cherokee Indians in the Southern Appalachians of North Carolina and Georgia. The sweet and aromatic candy roasters, along with the majority of foods we harvest—both wild and cultivated—are representative of the long history of this land and the Indigenous and enslaved who tended it over the centuries. Reconciling the depth of the harrowing history in Virginia can be overwhelming, but I also believe there is a profound opportunity to recognize, honor, and seek out the truth. There is unending wisdom held by the individuals and peoples who stewarded this land. They were the true innovators and protectors, and in order to preserve their traditions, we must acknowledge this painful history and give credit where it is due.

Winter

In 2019, winter was bizarrely warm. The grass grew four inches in January, grasshoppers and flies emerged from their dormancy, and, for the first time, the ponds did not freeze. Becoming a close observer of the land also means an increased awareness of the way our climate is changing on our watch. This is what fuels our work to sequester carbon from our atmosphere and put it back into our soils. We move the cattle multiple times a day, mimicking the ancient grazing patterns of the herbivores that coevolved with the grasses and vegetation on this land. This management, often referred to as holistic management, gives the vegetation the fertility and pruning it needs to thrive and photosynthesize effectively. Biodiversity returns, water infiltrates, and carbon is released through root exudates in the soil. It's a continuous learning process, but witnessing positive change is the ultimate form of encouragement and gives us the energy to keep going.

Cooking is . . .

"Difficult when you have young kids and no time to meal plan or shop for ingredients, let alone cook."

—Sophie
Oakland, CA

"The chore I'd rather do over just about any other household task; a connection to my grandmother and mother as well as my husband and children; something I'm proud to have mastered."

—Regina
Williamstown, MA

"A way to show people I care about them."

—Anne
Lyman, SC

"As someone who cooks at home and professionally, I do sometimes feel the societal burden of what it means to be a woman who spends time in the kitchen. I'm glad that we are coming into a time where we can let go of that line of thinking and really embrace what is happening for many women in the kitchen creatively, energetically, and self-care wise."

—Ellie
Brooklyn, NY

"Sometimes I love to cook, and other times it is exhausting because I am tired and I just don't want to do it, but it has to be done. I also grew up baking, but I was forced to go gluten-free thirteen years ago when I got very, very sick. As grateful as I am to know how to feel well, giving up wheat forever changed my life and the way that I relate to food. It also changed the way I feel about social situations involving foods and restaurants. I cook for my family because we can all feel safe and nourished. I don't find that anywhere else because there is always risk."

—Brenda
Lafayette, IN

"A way to be creative, to serve my family, and to honor our traditions and our relatives, even those who have passed on."

—Joan
Calabash, NC

"I felt perversely compelled to take this survey on behalf of women like me, who aren't really cooks at all. My mom was quite put upon to feed five picky and allergy-ridden kids (to say nothing of my dad), and sighing was a common sound in the kitchen. It can be a thankless task that seems to gain invisibility by virtue of how often and automatically meals happen. I am grateful to my mom for powering through! Not everyone has the inclination or luxury to access the 'joy of cooking.'"

—Karen
New York, NY

"For me, cooking is something that ties me so beautifully to the generations of women who came before me. I learned from my mom, and she learned from her mom, and on and on up the line. Now I am teaching my girls to cook, and we are tasting the same things that our foremothers tasted one night at their own tables."

—Heather
San Francisco, CA

"A part of the day that I look forward to sharing with my daughter. It's a time to talk about more than just cooking."

—Michelle
Cookeville, TN

"Food is a unifier. I believe it nourishes much more than one's body."

—Kate
Portland, OR

Amanda Saab

Born to Lebanese immigrants, Amanda Saab was raised near Detroit, which is home to one of the nation's largest Muslim populations. Saab pursued a career as a social worker, but she frequently found herself spending time in the kitchen as a way to relieve stress, guided by her mother's and grandmother's recipes.

In 2015, she competed on season six of MasterChef, *becoming the first woman in hijab to appear on an American cooking show. Though she was well received, she was also the target of hate speech. The following year, Saab and her husband created Dinner with Your Muslim Neighbor, inviting strangers into their home for a home-cooked meal and conversation as a way to "dispel the misconceptions many people have, give insight into our day-to-day lives as American Muslims, [and] create a better sense of community and understanding."*

During a Dinner with Your Muslim Neighbor that was hosted during the month of Ramadan, a woman named Jane* arrived at our door with a gift in hand. Jane was nervous—I could tell by her jitteriness and rosy cheeks. She was polite but reserved and didn't say very much.

The dinner menu that evening was a traditional Lebanese iftar, or breaking-of-fast meal, which included lentil soup; fattoush with crunchy pita bread; hummus that took two days to make; rice pilaf with toasted nuts, dried fruit, and parsley; beef kefta; and pickles and bread. For dessert, I served my baklava cheesecake: graham cracker crust, cream cheese filling spiced with cardamom and rose water, layers of flaky phyllo dough, and nuts topping it all.

The meal was wonderful. We passed and shared dishes throughout the evening, going

back for seconds and thirds. The conversation had a natural flow that went on for several hours, but Jane had not spoken much, despite efforts to engage her. It was about 1 a.m. when Jane finally spoke up.

She cleared her throat and, with the encouraging nod of her friend, said, "I have something to share." Without pause, she continued, "I was Islamophobic. I was afraid of Syrian refugees moving into my community and I feared they were going to harm me and my children. But I have been working with a therapist and my pastor and when I learned of these dinners, I knew I had to come."

It was silent for a moment before I was able to speak through the slow stream of tears running down my face. I thanked Jane for being honest and brave about exposing her feelings, and her ability to allow herself to be vulnerable. Creating a judgment-free environment where people who were once strangers are able to share intimate thoughts and feelings has been the most profound accomplishment of these dinners. This encounter proved that connection, community, and gathering over a meal are significant and can make a difference. This alone motivates and encourages us to host more dinners.

*Name and identifying details have been changed.

Rosio Sanchez

A FIRST-GENERATION Mexican American, Rosio Sanchez fell in love with baking as a teen, testing recipes from magazines to satisfy her sweet tooth and seeking out Mexican specialties like paletas, tres leches cake, and corn esquites from street vendors in her Chicago neighborhood. Her kitchen experiments became a window into other countries, cultures, and cuisines, inspiring her to pursue a career in food.

After culinary school, she landed a position as a pastry sous chef at WD-50, Wylie Dufresne's modernist restaurant in New York, and later worked her way through some of Europe's finest restaurants. While in Spain, she was approached by a colleague and fellow chef at René Redzepi's famed Copenhagen restaurant, Noma, about an open position there. Sanchez seized the coveted opportunity and worked for five years as the restaurant's head pastry chef and in its experimental test kitchen.

Sanchez's time at Noma—famous for its erudite, experimental focus on foraging and hyperlocal Scandinavian ingredients—was her primer in wild treasures like moss and gooseberry and processes like fermentation. It was a creative and

ABOVE

Strawberry and elderflower paleta with habanero glaze, one of a variety of flavors served at Hija de Sanchez

challenging role, but as much as she enjoyed it, Sanchez felt compelled to connect more deeply with her heritage and Mexican food. In 2015, she opened a contemporary taqueria, Hija de Sanchez, in Copenhagen's centrally located Torvehallerne market. "I had to take [my] experience and practice it in my own life and get out of my comfort zone," she says.

The taqueria introduced bold new flavors to a Nordic community that had little to no experience with Mexican cuisine. After only a year, Hija de Sanchez was hailed as the best street food in Europe; it became so popular that Sanchez opened a second location in the city's meatpacking district.

In 2017, she expanded her business by opening Sanchez Cantina, a sit-down restaurant that marked a significant turning point in her career and mindset. "It was when this restaurant opened that I finally accepted who I am, and it shows in the food that we make,"

Sanchez says. The menu integrates Mexican- and Scandinavian-inspired cuisines, symbolizing two sides of her identity.

For all of her restaurants, Sanchez sources native varieties of corn and peppers from independent farmers in Oaxaca, Mexico, helping support their communities and adding depth and unique flavor to the food she creates half a world away. She is equally passionate about using Nordic ingredients— such as sea buckthorn, elderflower, and local wild herbs and seaweeds— and Mexican-style cheeses that she has made by a local dairy company.

Copenhagen remains home for now, though travel and adventure still beckon. "I think I have so much more of Mexico and the world to explore, personally and professionally," she says. "It's inspiring that a Chicana girl born from Mexican immigrants can have such a life as I have had. That our work matters to so many people gives me hope."

"Anything is possible as long as there is honesty and passion and you always listen to your gut feeling."

ESSAY BY

Polina Chesnakova

Polina Chesnakova is a food writer, recipe developer, and cooking instructor based in Seattle. In 1992, when she was just a newborn, her family immigrated to the United States from the former Soviet republic of Georgia during the Soviet Union's collapse. Her work and her food blog, Chesnok, are a celebration of her multicultural heritage.

Dedakatsi

From her perch atop the Sololaki Ridge, Georgia's most famous woman—and protector—proudly stands sixty-five feet tall and looks down over the ancient city of Tbilisi. Her left hand lifts a bowl of wine in greeting, and her right hand grips a sword in warning. Named Kartlis Deda, or Mother of Georgia, she was erected in 1958 as an embodiment of the national character: a hospitality that knows no bounds and a fierce pride in the country's freedom and strength. For decades, the monument has also stood as a reminder to all women of their familial and national duties to provide for and protect their home.

Seeing women as devoted caretakers above all else is a concept deeply rooted in the Georgian patriarchal narrative, even today.

But this imperative was brought to a whole new level during and following World War II, when women had to take on the role of breadwinner while their husbands were away fighting. Thousands of men never came home, and the ones who did returned physically and mentally maimed, unable to fully or properly care for their families again. What other options did these mothers, wives, sisters, and daughters have but to continue carrying out their familial duties—even if this responsibility verged on the self-sacrificial? So, they labored on—cooking, cleaning, working, and persevering—and eventually these resilient women became known as the dedakatsi, or "mother-man."

This phenomenon continued through the remainder of the

The Kartlis Deda
monument in
Tbilisi, Georgia

Kaukasis the Cookbook: A Culinary Journey Through Georgia, Azerbaijan & Beyond. She described coming across the concept and history of the dedakatsi. "For me," said Hercules, who was born in Ukraine, "it was the most incredible discovery. I met so many women like that who have nothing to do with the feminism movement. They don't know what it is, but they are that—personified."

Hercules reminded me of the strong, independent women in my own life: my mother and her six sisters, who were born and raised in Tbilisi. They learned from a very early age how to get by and be content with very little; that life owed them nothing; and that hard work always paid off. As they grew older, each sister followed her own path, but their familial ties and sense of obligation to each other remained strong. Eventually, five of them (including my mother) fled the country together in the chaotic wake of the Soviet Union's collapse.

These dedakatsi taught me perseverance, willpower, and sisterhood. But the most formative lesson I gleaned from them was the power of food. Images from my childhood of my mother standing at the stove stirring a big pot of stew or at the counter chopping cilantro will forever be ingrained

twentieth century as social and economic turmoil racked the Soviet-bloc country. The women of this new generation were forced to find creative ways to generate income—hawking goods such as secondhand clothes or homemade cakes on the streets, for example—while men continued to sit at home without jobs. Time and time again, in response to male defeatism, these determined dedakatsi rose to the challenge.

I first heard the term "mother-man" while listening to an interview with London-based chef and author Olia Hercules discussing her book

"My mother and aunts learned to assimilate Georgian cuisine into their everyday [life] while staying true to their Russian roots by cooking dishes like this green sorrel borscht. By teaching me how to prepare this soup along with the rest of their Georgian and Russian repertoire, they pass down a fusion of flavors, ingredients, and foodways that are unique to our family's immigration experience. Sorrel isn't widely available where I grew up in Rhode Island, so instead of letting go of green borscht completely, my aunt Olga chose to grow the plant herself!"

LEFT

Chesnakova's tangy green borscht, made with a heap of sorrel, potatoes, eggs, and carrots and finished with sour cream and herbs

in my mind. As I grew older, I found myself being drawn to the kitchen and spending more time alongside her and my aunts. I came to see how a simple meal made from scratch not only filled our needs on the most elemental level, but also comforted and united us. Whether we were rolling khachapuri or grating beets for borscht, we were keeping a food heritage alive that restored a bit of the life they had left behind, while paving the way for new traditions.

As these women continue to share their knowledge with me, I preserve it by sharing it with others through my writing. Genuine interest from others has encouraged my mother and aunts to see their heritage in a new light. What was once a dull familial duty and necessity is now approached with an eagerness, passion, and pride I never witnessed growing up.

This dedication has redefined what it means to be a dedakatsi in the twenty-first century: a woman whose strength lies not in her ability to take on "manly" tasks, but in her willingness to face life's obstacles head-on. Whose value and sense of worth stem not from her finesse with a broom or a rolling pin, but from the passions and aspirations that drive her to do and be better. Who finds independence in fully and abundantly loving herself— and letting self-love set her free. Dedakatsi exist not only in Georgia, but throughout the world, in all walks of life. We inspire, encourage, and look after each other in a way that I know would make Kartlis Deda proud.

Adapted from "Dedakatsi: The Unsung Feminist" by Polina Chesnakova, *Comestible* 7 (2018), with permission. Copyright © 2021 by Polina Chesnakova.

How can women help each other grow and succeed in the food industry?

"I recognize that my success is because of the hard work of women and people of color who came before me, and I always remember to acknowledge that publicly. I look to those who came before me to seek knowledge, and I seek to build community with other women and people of color in the food world so that we can lift each other up."

—**Reem Assil**
chef and owner of Reem's California,
entrepreneur, and activist
Oakland and San Francisco, CA

"As a boss, I have always intentionally worked to recruit and hire women and people of color and make sure they are supported in their work environment. I have developed relationships with women chefs both older and younger than me to form the type of bonds, camaraderie, and informal mentorship that is necessary for all of our success. And I have used and will continue to use my platform to lift up other women in all industries. One thing we can all do is remember that we are not each other's competition, we are each other's success."

—**Preeti Mistry**
chef, entrepreneur, speaker, and activist
Oakland, CA

"Taking the time to seek out women who share your values, collaborating with them whenever possible and celebrating their successes. For me, this means bringing women food professionals into our kitchens as instructors so they can share their own stories and knowledge, setting a positive example for our students. It's placing students in kitchens run by women and showing them how kitchen culture can be positive while still demanding and exacting."

—**Jodi Liano**
founder and director of
San Francisco Cooking School,
cooking instructor, and author
San Francisco, CA

"Workers have to understand the full context of their environment in order to build and exercise power (and empower each other), and that's why we build the team's business and leadership skills and provide transparency in our financial reporting. We're trying to break down the barriers between employees, managers, and owners by putting us all on the same team so that when we succeed, we succeed together."

—Irene Li
chef and owner of Mei Mei Restaurant
Boston, MA

"The best thing to do is listen to women, to hear what they love and are passionate about. When I first told one of my best friends that I wanted to open a bakery, she asked me how it would look, what would be on the menu, where it would be—very direct, probing questions that made me feel accountable to her. The more we do this for each other, the more we will see women move forward."

—Angela Garbacz
pastry chef and owner of Goldenrod Pastries and
founder of Empower Through Flour
Lincoln, NE

"I see women supporting other women the most when we're *all* around a table. There's magic there, and we can use it to spark the changes we want to see, for women within the world of food and beverage and for those outside of it."

—Maryam Ahmed
consultant, coach, and creator of the
Diversity in Wine Leadership Forum
Napa, CA

"Commitment to diversity doesn't just mean hiring as many minorities (including women here) and sticking them in the lowest-paying positions— it means purposely finding them leadership positions to elevate their equitability."

—June Rodil
master sommelier and partner at
Goodnight Hospitality and June's All Day
Houston, TX

"I think the first step is being honest about our stories. It's easy to hide our problems in favor of seeming confident, poised, and in control. Being honest about our struggles—whether they be related to gender, race, health, performance, money, assault, etc.— gives us more power, not less."

—Jane Lopes
sommelier and cofounder of
LEGEND Wine Imports
Los Angeles, CA

Jessica B. Harris

CELEBRATED CULINARY historian, author, scholar, journalist, and educator Jessica B. Harris has dedicated her life to researching and chronicling the cuisines and foodways of the African diaspora and is widely recognized for her unparalleled knowledge on the subject.

In the 1970s, Harris traveled to West Africa while working on her doctoral dissertation and to the Caribbean as the first Black woman travel editor for *Essence* magazine. These experiences gave her a taste of the similarities between the regions' cuisines, igniting her passion for studying African American food, history, and culture.

Throughout her decades-long career, Harris has received numerous honors for her trailblazing research and writing, and in 2012, she helped conceptualize the award-winning Sweet Home Café at the Smithsonian National Museum of African American History and Culture in Washington, DC. Harris retired in 2018 after fifty years of teaching at Queens College, but she continues to write, consult, and lecture in the United States and abroad. She splits her time between Brooklyn, New Orleans, and Martha's Vineyard.

Chicken Yassa

Serves 4 to 6

Chicken yassa (poulet yassa or yassa ganar in French and Wolof, one of the languages of Senegal) was a linchpin dish for me. I first tasted it in 1972 on my first trip to the African continent, and it was indeed love at first bite. I learned how to cook it from friends and recipes, substituting the broiler for the feu malgache (wood-fired grill), over which it traditionally gets an infusion of wood smoke. I consider it my good-luck recipe and have included a version of it in almost all my cookbooks.

¼ cup freshly squeezed lemon juice (from 1 or 2 lemons)

4 large onions, cut into very thin slices

Salt and freshly ground black pepper, to taste

⅛ teaspoon minced fresh habanero or other hot chile pepper, plus 1 whole habanero chile pepper, pricked with the tines of a fork

¼ cup plus 1 tablespoon peanut oil

One whole chicken (about 3½ pounds), gizzard discarded, cut into serving pieces

½ cup pimiento-stuffed olives

4 carrots, trimmed and cut crosswise into thin slices

1 tablespoon Dijon mustard

White rice, for serving

1 Combine the lemon juice, onions, salt, pepper, minced habanero, and ¼ cup of the peanut oil in a gallon-size, resealable plastic bag. Add the chicken pieces and seal the bag; massage to coat evenly. Marinate the chicken in the refrigerator for at least 2 hours.

2 Position the top oven rack 4 to 6 inches from the broiler element; preheat the broiler. Line a baking sheet with aluminum foil. Transfer the chicken pieces from the marinade to the baking sheet, skin side up. (Reserve the onions and the marinade.) Broil the chicken for 8 to 10 minutes, then turn the pieces over and broil for another 8 minutes, until the chicken is browned on both sides (it will not be cooked through).

3 Meanwhile, heat the remaining tablespoon of peanut oil in a large Dutch oven over medium-low heat. Add the reserved onions, shaking off as much of the marinade as possible, and cook for about 20 minutes, until they are translucent and tender. Add the remaining marinade and stir well; increase the heat to medium and cook, stirring occasionally, until the liquid comes to a low boil.

❹ Add the broiled chicken pieces, pricked habanero, olives, carrots, mustard, and ½ cup water, stirring to mix well. Once the liquid returns to a boil, reduce the heat to medium-low, cover, and cook for 20 minutes, or until the chicken has cooked through. Taste occasionally, and remove the whole habanero when the desired spice level has been reached. Serve hot over white rice.

Amanda Cohen

Amanda Cohen is the chef and owner of New York City's award-winning Dirt Candy, a vegetable-focused restaurant that opened in 2008. When she's not at her restaurant, Cohen competes on Iron Chef Canada *and serves on the boards of Women Chefs and Restaurateurs and Women in Hospitality United.*

The Invisible Women

When I opened Dirt Candy, I put everything on the line. I tried to cover all the angles, carefully calculating staffing costs, estimating a budget that would keep my doors open, picking a name that would stand out in a crowded marketplace. I considered every variable except one: The press noticed my gender before they noticed my food, again and again.

I got attention for speaking out about the lack of coverage for women chefs before I was actually covered as a woman chef. Even today, four years after I opened a bigger and better Dirt Candy, I'm still waiting for a single mainstream review. When so many fine-dining restaurants are struggling to survive, press coverage keeps the doors open. And for the past twenty years, women have been placed in a special category where they receive coverage only after the "real" chefs (read: boys) have their turn.

But before then, women chefs used to be everywhere. The Chu Niang were the rock star lady chefs of China's Song Dynasty. Josefina Velázquez de León singlehandedly preserved Mexico's vast regional cuisine in her cookbooks. Edna Lewis brought Southern food to New York City. Sylvia Woods built a soul food empire out of her Harlem restaurant, Sylvia's. Leslie Revsin was the first woman chef in the Waldorf-Astoria's eighty-year history, but after that, not a single French restaurant in New York City would hire her, so she opened her own. Dione Lucas was the first chef to have a television show.

These women were largely erased. When Alain Ducasse opened his first restaurant in New York City in 2000, the *Los Angeles Times*, CNN, and other press outlets reported that he was the first chef in history to hold six simultaneous Michelin stars, completely overlooking Eugénie Brazier, one of the grandmothers of French cuisine, who had already achieved this very feat back in 1933. When we make the boys look small, they write us out of the picture.

In 1999, food columnist Marian Burros wrote a piece for the *New York Times* lamenting that some of the great women chefs of the '80s and '90s—Anne Rosenzweig, Sally Darr, Diane Forley, Katy Sparks, and Debra Ponzek—were gone, and wondering who would replace them. The answer: no one. I blame Anthony Bourdain's *Kitchen Confidential*, published in 2000. His book made cooking cool, but it also implied that kitchens were all about tattoos and heroin, rowdy binge-drinking, and loud boys. The press, always desperate to look cool, agreed: Kitchens had no room for women unless they wanted to drape dead pigs over their shoulders and brag about their scars. Food coverage became

about excess and large-format feasts. *New York Magazine* panted over Mario Batali's holiday meal at the Spotted Pig in 2007: twenty-one indulgent courses, closing with "celebratory cake served by scantily clad babes." Women got crowded out of the picture, becoming little more than tokens. Between 2000 and 2018, *Food & Wine* selected 208 "Best New Chefs in America." Only thirty-five of them were women, and only nine of them were women of color. Being a woman made you roadkill on a testosterone highway that celebrated excess and self-indulgence, which exacerbated the toxic swamp of rape and sexual harassment. Now we're standing in the rubble, wondering what comes next.

Good.

I've never been more excited to be a chef than I am today. The organizations that hand out food awards are either collapsing or losing all credibility because they have aided and abetted egregious discrimination for years, and are totally unprepared for the reckoning that has arrived. Writers are fighting with their editors to file stories about women chefs, not because they're women, but because they haven't gotten enough attention for their food. We have a whole new generation of young women chefs who won't stay quiet, demanding the attention that is their due.

But let's remember that they stand on the shoulders of the women who bridged that twenty-year gap, women like Anita Lo, Barbara Lynch, Traci Des Jardins, Jody Adams, and Sara Jenkins. Women who did the work but didn't get the praise. Women who worked the line while their male colleagues went to parties and committed sexual harassment. Women who weren't asked their opinions by the press or invited to be on panels. Women who kept the lights on and the stoves lit. Who turned out food that will stand the test of time. Women who gave jobs to other women. We must constantly celebrate the women who came before us so they won't be forgotten once more, and we can never take our progress for granted. As we've learned again and again, it can all disappear in the flick of a pen.

What is the best thing about being mobile?

"Being able to travel and see how our product does in different areas. We started Lumpia City in San Diego (Alexa's hometown), a city that's open to a wide variety of cultures, innovation, and fresh ideas, not to mention a big Filipino/Asian presence. When we made the decision to move to Milwaukee, Wisconsin (Sam's hometown), one of our biggest concerns was how our food would be accepted, given that Milwaukee is a smaller and more traditional city with not much Filipino influence. Even though we serve something that is virtually unknown in the Midwest, our fusion recipes display familiarity in a fun and creative way that intrigues people, whether or not they know what a lumpia is. We have since gained confidence that wherever we may go, our product will do well."

—**Alexa Reyes &
Samantha Klimaszewski**
co-chefs and co-owners of Lumpia City
Milwaukee, WI

"Over the last ten years, being mobile has allowed us to bring our 'everyday aloha' to the greater Seattle area and build long-term relationships with our customers. Many were introduced to us at lunch or at a food truck event. Later, they visited us, often bringing friends and family, as we expanded to brick-and-mortar restaurants. Our food truck remains the mobile ambassador of our company, and we are so grateful for the reach this has provided us, both geographically and over time."

—**Roz Edison** (COO) **& Kamala Saxton**
cofounders of Marination
Seattle, WA

"I believe mobility and flexibility are the future of the food industry. It is the best way for me to raise more awareness, go places, be outside of the box, and reach more diners."

—**Siska Silitonga**
chef and owner of ChiliCali
San Francisco, CA

"There's something magical about running up to a truck filled with delicious food—I think it hearkens back to the ice cream trucks of childhood. It's so fun to interact with guests from a truck window and see the same folks every week. Knowing they are waiting for us is always a great feeling."

—**Irene Li**
chef and owner of Mei Mei Restaurant
Boston, MA

"The ability to pull up to someone's house for a birthday party, wedding venue, or park for Sunday funday and serve them delicious food is amazing! A mobile kitchen does not allow for a lot of space, so it forces creativity."

—**Ikeisha Fields**
chef and owner of Soul Skillet Street Kitchen
San Francisco, CA

What do you love most about the direct interaction with your customers?

"Seeing how many of our followers will travel outside of their area just to support us and get our food. Social media outlets are huge for us! We're constantly posting about upcoming events and interacting with our followers to get them excited about coming to see us."

—**Alexa Reyes &
Samantha Klimaszewski**
co-chefs and co-owners of Lumpia City
Milwaukee, WI

"A food truck is like having an open kitchen. We are lucky because our truck is designed with one very large

window taking up the entire side of the truck. This allows us to see and interact with our customers throughout their transaction, which is interesting for them and our team alike."

—**Roz Edison** (COO) **& Kamala Saxton**
cofounders of Marination
Seattle, WA

"My pop-up dinners and food stall give me the opportunity to interact with my diners in an intimate environment. I can test a new menu or recipes on them and get direct feedback. My pop-up dinners are where my community meets, shares stories, and relates to one another. By feeding them I nourish myself and feel more alive."

—**Siska Silitonga**
chef and owner of ChiliCali
San Francisco, CA

"It can be so much more casual—guests have lower or different expectations. I also love that there is no barrier between front of house and back of house."

—**Irene Li**
chef and owner of Mei Mei Restaurant
Boston, MA

"The feeling you get when you watch someone take a bite of their meal—their eyes close and their body melts with joy and appreciation for something tasty—is priceless."

—**Ikeisha Fields**
chef and owner of Soul Skillet Street Kitchen
San Francisco, CA

Cristina Martinez

IN 2009, Cristina Martinez fled her hometown of Capulhuac, Mexico, for the United States to escape domestic violence and earn money for her daughter's education. She found work as a pastry chef in Philadelphia, but she was fired after her employer discovered that she was undocumented. Longing for a connection to Mexico, Martinez began cooking what she knew best: her family's generations-old recipe for lamb barbacoa. She paired the slow-cooked meat with her homemade tortillas and sold tacos to her neighbors, first from her apartment and later from a food cart.

Encouraged by the community's warm response, Martinez and her husband, chef Ben Miller, opened a restaurant—South Philly Barbacoa—in 2015. One year later, *Bon Appétit* named it one of the top ten best new restaurants in America. In 2018, Martinez was featured on Netflix's *Chef's Table*, and not long after, she was nominated for a James Beard Foundation Award for Best Chef: Mid-Atlantic. In 2020, she built on these successes, opening a new restaurant called Casa Mexico.

Passionate about using their platform to champion immigrant rights in their community, Martinez and Miller founded the Popular Alliance for Undocumented Workers' Rights, an organization that raises awareness of the adversities faced by immigrant workers.

As Martinez likes to say: "Food doesn't know borders." It is a philosophy that has guided her through building a life in the United States and creating welcoming spaces in which people of all backgrounds can come together, enjoy her food, and find common ground.

Martinez's Tortillas, Step by Step

1 Martinez and Miller work with local farmers who grow and supply the restaurant with heirloom varieties of corn—the essential ingredient.

2 Once harvested, the corn undergoes nixtamalization, an ancient Mesoamerican process that boosts the corn's nutritional value and allows it to be easily ground into grain. First the corn is soaked in limewater, then it is hulled, refrigerated, and left to sit overnight.

> "I learned to make tortillas by watching my grandma near the tlecuil when I was six years old. For me, it is not a tradition. It's a robust profession that has been passed down over many years from our Indigenous ancestors."

❸ The corn is rinsed and ground using a stone mill. The resulting nixtamal (ground corn) is made into masa (dough), shaped into small, flat rounds, and then flattened in a tortilla press.

❹ The dough rounds are cooked on a hot comal (griddle). Martinez places the fresh tortillas in a woven basket covered with a napkin to keep them hot until ready to eat.

LEFT

A plate of lamb barbacoa tacos. "In a weekend, [we make] 11,000 tortillas, one by one," says Martinez.

How do you balance your work and personal life?

"My boyfriend is also in the industry, and we share the understanding that we are committed to work. Luckily we also share days off, so we spend all the time we can together. Taking extra time off to visit my family and dogs in California is hard. But prioritizing is the key, and making a promise to prioritize your personal life is the first step."

—Mimi Mendoza
pastry chef at Senia
Honolulu, HI

"I have been trying really hard to say no a lot more than I have in the past and to only say yes to things that bring me happiness and are meaningful to me or our company. Practicing this is tough, but it's helpful to ask myself if I would say yes to the opportunity if it were tonight, because of course when it's far off in my calendar it's super easy to imagine that I will be happy to do it."

—Renee Erickson
chef and co-owner of Sea Creatures restaurants
Seattle, WA

"I have no balance or line between my professional cooking life and my personal life! Some people would hate that, but I just don't."

—Katie Workman
food writer, recipe developer, and author
New York, NY

"Juggling two small kids, our businesses, and all of the travel that my husband and I do is challenging. We are just now having conversations about how to restore a sense of sanity in our lives. We are going to try to find our balance through extended summer vacations, so we won't feel quite as guilty about working like crazy throughout the school year. I also try to schedule time with friends so I don't turn into a hermit running from home to work and back every day."

—Katie Button
executive chef and CEO of Katie Button Restaurants
Asheville, NC

"I have a rule: Outside of the harvest season, I take my kids to school every day. With my daily workload, I could stay at work very late, but I try to leave early enough so that I can have dinner with them and put them to bed. Then if I need to finish working at home, I do that."

—Ana Diogo-Draper
director of winemaking at Artesa Vineyards & Winery
Napa, CA

"I haven't figured that out. I've gone from one extreme to another."

—Anita Lo
chef, culinary tour guide, and author
New York, NY

Barbara Lynch

CHEF BARBARA LYNCH got her first kitchen job at a local rectory at age thirteen. One of seven children, Lynch was raised by her single mother in a housing project in South Boston. "Let's just say that no one expected much from me, and I certainly didn't expect much from myself. My home economics teacher showed me a way I could succeed through cooking and gave me the tools I needed to do so," says Lynch.

In her early twenties, she worked with some of Boston's most acclaimed chefs before traveling through Italy, where she learned about Italian cooking from local women. When Lynch returned to the United States, she became the executive chef of a small trattoria in Boston called Galleria Italiana, where she earned national recognition.

In 1998, Lynch opened her first restaurant in Boston—No. 9 Park, an ode to regionally inspired Italian and French cuisine—to rave reviews. In the two decades since, she formed the Barbara Lynch Collective, a group of seven restaurants, including award-winning No. 9 Park and Menton.

Lynch remains deeply connected to the Boston community and supports young entrepreneurs and chefs by offering benefits, training, and advancement opportunities to her employees. "I want to help give kids the same independence that I found through cooking," she reflects. "I knew if I could cook I would always have a job! It's important that they know they can do anything they want if they have a vision."

"People were skeptical that I would make it out of Southie. Sometimes I still have a hard time believing it. Knowing that I overcame my own doubt and the doubt of other people keeps me strong when I'm feeling vulnerable and drives me to empower others to do the same."

BELOW

Lynch in her kitchen in Gloucester, Massachusetts. "When I've been traveling a lot, I make a recipe that always resets my system. It's pretty simple, but incredibly delicious: ceci beans, lentils, porcini mushrooms, fenugreek, and crushed red chili flakes," she says.

Hillel Echo-Hawk

CHEF, CATERER, AND educator Hillel Echo-Hawk was born and raised in Delta Junction, Alaska, but she is a member of the Pawnee Nation of Oklahoma. Throughout her childhood, Echo-Hawk and her family spent weekends in nearby Mentasta Lake, an Athabaskan village, where they watched and learned from Katie John, an Ahtna elder, matriarch, and activist who dedicated her life to fighting for Indigenous food sovereignty and hunting and fishing rights. Eventually, the family was adopted through her mother, the Athabaskan way, expanding Echo-Hawk's knowledge of and passion for Indigenous cooking and wellness.

Years later, Echo-Hawk settled in Seattle to attend culinary school. After graduating, she cooked in several of the city's restaurants and joined I-Collective, a group of Indigenous chefs and activists who organize and lead initiatives focused on health, social justice, and the preservation of Indigenous foodways.

In 2018, inspired to serve the Indigenous community and highlight its traditional foods, Echo-Hawk founded Birch Basket Catering. In her cooking and classes, she highlights pre-colonization Indigenous ingredients and traditions with modern cooking techniques, sharing the stories of her people and the land and drawing on a collective ancient wisdom. "Food should not only feed the body, but the spirit of the entire community," says Echo-Hawk.

BELOW AND PAGE 80

Sunflowers, fireweed, forget-me-nots, and tundra rose—plants that symbolize Echo-Hawk's Pawnee and Alaskan heritage

Sage Buffalo Meatballs
with Sweet Potato Puree

Serves 6

Buffalo was a main source of my tribe's diet for thousands of years before colonization. Twice a year, the entire tribe would go on a hunt and get all the meat that would be necessary to feed them. It was only when we were forced onto the reservation that we stopped eating it regularly and our diet began to change. I created this recipe in honor of and with the guidance of my ancestors.

❶ Preheat the oven to 400°F. Line a rimmed baking sheet with parchment paper.

❷ In a large bowl, combine the ground buffalo, 1½ cups of the quinoa, the onion, the sage, and 1 teaspoon salt. Mix until evenly distributed.

❸ In a small skillet, heat a splash of oil and fry a small portion of the meatball mixture to see if it holds together. If it falls apart, add more quinoa to the raw mixture until it holds together. Taste the sample cooked meatball and adjust the seasoning in the rest of the mixture, if necessary. Once you're ready, start rolling the meatball mixture into 1½- to 2-inch balls and place them on the prepared baking sheet with at least 1 inch between meatballs. Once the tray is full, place it in the oven and bake until the meatballs are browned and cooked through, about 20 minutes.

❹ Meanwhile, bring 2 quarts of water to a boil in a medium-size pot over high heat. Add a pinch of salt. Add the sweet potato and garlic clove to the pot and boil for 12 to 15 minutes, or until the sweet potato is very tender.

1 pound ground buffalo

2 cups cooked quinoa, cooled

1 cup diced white onion

4 teaspoons dried sage

1 teaspoon salt, plus more as needed

Canola oil or other neutral oil, for frying

1 cup peeled and diced sweet potato

1 clove garlic, peeled

5 Using a heatproof measuring cup, reserve 1 cup of the cooking liquid. Drain the remaining liquid. Place the sweet potato and garlic clove in a blender or a food processor and puree until smooth; be careful not to overblend. Thin with some of the reserved liquid if needed, but the puree should not be too runny; aim for the consistency of a thick sauce. Taste and adjust the seasoning.

6 To serve, spoon puree onto each of six plates and arrange meatballs atop or alongside the puree.

"Sunflowers are the Pawnee's Fourth Sister. They are planted along with squash, corn, and beans to protect them from the wind and predators. They add nutrients to the soil, and every part of them is edible. They grow taller than our corn and help with cross-pollination as well. We don't plant without them."

"I get happiness from seeing people's eyes when they eat the food I've cooked. That feeling when you can light up someone's soul with something you've prepared, that is a privilege and an honor."

—Asma Khan
chef, restaurateur, and author

Deborah A. Harris

As a professor of sociology at Texas State University in San Marcos, Texas, Deborah A. Harris explores inequality in the food system and the impact on women. Her 2015 book, Taking the Heat: Women Chefs and Gender Inequality in the Professional Kitchen, *coauthored with Patti Giuffre, delves into the deep-rooted gender biases that permeate the professional culinary world and offers ideas for working toward a more equal future.*

Five Years Later: Are Women Chefs Still Taking the Heat?

In 2015, only about 20 percent of head and executive chefs were women. Why? What we found was a complex set of issues that included:

→ A history of professional chefs excluding women in order to better differentiate professional cooking from home cooking to raise the status of the career

→ A workplace culture that valued macho (and often abusive) behavior that was unwelcoming to women

→ A food-focused media that described men as innovative empire builders and women as homey cooks

→ An industry that made it difficult to combine work and family responsibilities

Since then, many people have asked if things are getting better for women chefs. On the surface, it's easy to argue that conditions haven't improved, as most statistics about women chefs remain unchanged. It takes many years to see cultural and ideological transformations, but we are already starting to see indicators of change:

→ The amount of criticism generated when another list of "Best Chefs" is published with few, if any, women suggests more attention is being paid to inclusive representation, including for women of color, who face additional barriers to success in the culinary world.

→ Media representation is becoming more balanced, with a focus on women who are setting new workplace standards in the culinary industry. This representation has expanded to include more women of color and women who work outside of traditional fine-dining establishments.

→ The #MeToo era and the rise in the number of men chefs and restaurant owners accused of sexual harassment and abuse has allowed us to finally acknowledge and demand change regarding some of the terrible behavior that has long been swept under the rug.

→ There is less acceptance of inequities and there are more people speaking out on how to reshape the professional kitchen. These conversations and actions are going beyond gender to also include race, ethnicity, sexuality, and more.

→ The James Beard Foundation's Women's Leadership Programs provide mentorship and entrepreneurial training to women who want to build their own empires in the food industry.

→ Women in Hospitality United hosts Solution Sprints around the country to identify potential solutions to problems women face in the industry, like sexual harassment and the gender pay gap.

→ Annual women-centered conferences like Cherry Bombe and FAB provide opportunities for women to network and learn from one another.

→ When *Food & Wine* published its "19 Great Restaurants to Work For" in 2019, seventeen of the twenty-seven owners on the list were women. These women are dedicated to providing living wages and 401(k) plans, hosting anti-harassment and anti-bias trainings, providing health (including mental health) benefits, and offering opportunities for cross-training and internal promotions. These practices create more respectful and fair workplaces, which help improve the culinary industry for all workers.

The culinary industry is known for its creativity and problem-solving, and more people than ever are recognizing that as women continue to thrive, so too will the industry as a whole.

What are your most treasured kitchen objects?

"I follow my mother's tradition of using letters and postcards to bookmark recipes in my cookbooks. Decades of friendship and family history are intertwined with favorite recipes: a beloved aunt's family holiday card marks our favorite pancake recipe so we 'see' them often; a high-school friend's postcard from her first year of college marks a cake recipe that still reminds me of the feelings of early adulthood.... It's important to match the sender with the perfect recipe."

—**Kate**
Mount Desert Island, ME

"Recipes from people who brought meals to me when I had our first babies. I wasn't a good cook then, so I collected all those delicious recipes. Still use a good portion of them nearly thirty years later."

—**Laura**
Michigan

"I have my grandma's eggbeater, which I love. I also have a fondness for old kitchen gadgets. I love the design and high quality they all seem to have."

—**Pamela**
Richmond, CA

"My mom's old ceramic bread bowl, which I think was *her* mom's. It's big and lovely—they don't make them like that anymore!"

—Hannah
Montpelier, VT

"I have made my own granola for thirty years! The recipe is from a lodge above the Arctic Circle that our family visited. It is handwritten on the back of a postcard with the lodge pictured on the front."

—Janice
Indianapolis, IN

"I have some recipe cards and cookbooks that belonged to my mother, who passed away a number of years ago. Seeing her handwriting means the most to me and makes me remember the love she put into our favorite dishes and the meals we shared as a family.

"I also have a classic Pyrex pie plate that belonged to my mom and a rolling pin that was my grandmother's. Making a pie is kind of a labor of love anyway, but making it with these treasured items, I always feel very connected to them."

—Gera
Elk Rapids, MI

Robyn Sue Fisher

ROBYN SUE FISHER, founder and CEO of Smitten® Ice Cream, has always been a tinkerer. As children, she and her brother hunted for rocks in the woods, painted them, and sold them to neighborhood kids. During that time, she also experienced chronic stomach issues and underwent multiple surgeries. She remembers ice cream as an indulgence that represented pure joy amid these challenges. Fisher grew to cherish it so much that to this day, she jokes that she has two stomachs—one for ice cream, and one for everything else.

After college, Fisher felt burned out and lost in a corporate consulting job. She enrolled in business school at Stanford, where a course for start-up entrepreneurs inspired her to research mass production in the ice cream industry. She learned about the additives used to preserve products (they often sit on shelves for months), saw an opportunity,

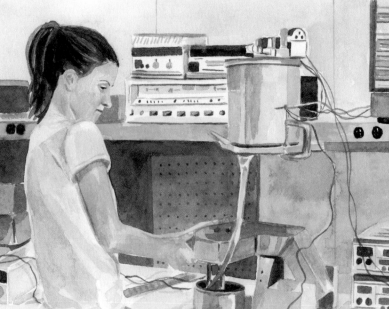

RIGHT

Fisher's red wagon, from which she sold her first batches of Smitten Ice Cream

Smitten's cookie dough ice cream with pretzels and chocolate chips (a bestseller) is always on the menu.

LEFT

Fisher tinkering with her Brrr machine prototype in 2009

rogue on the street than I did in any classroom," she says.

In 2011, Fisher opened Smitten's first brick-and-mortar shop in the city's Hayes Valley neighborhood. Smitten now has five locations in Northern California and owns six patents on the Brrr machine. Despite the company's growth, Fisher has not wavered from her primary vision of delivering joy to her customers: "The whole reason I have become 'the ice cream gal' is because I wanted to use technology to reconstruct and repair this beloved food category that is all about embracing and spreading joy. The smiles on people's faces are what make my day."

and embarked on a quest to build a better ice cream machine. Her penchant for tinkering came full circle.

Over the course of two years, with the help of a retired aerospace engineer, she developed the first prototype of her Brrr® machine. Using liquid nitrogen, the Brrr machine churns and freezes ingredients on the spot at a very cold temperature to create smooth, creamy ice cream without preservatives. When her prototype was up and running, Fisher took to the streets, hauling her invention around on a red wooden wagon to sell ice cream all over San Francisco. She quickly drew huge crowds, and she remembers this phase of Smitten's evolution fondly. "I learned more selling ice cream

Anita Lo

ANITA LO IS a chef and author who grew up in Birmingham, Michigan. While studying French at Columbia University's language institute in Paris, Lo became smitten with France's food and culture, and she promised herself she would return someday to pursue her passion for cooking. Once she arrived back in the United States, she worked as a pantry chef, or garde-manger, at Bouley in New York, but a year later she went back to Paris to attend culinary school and take apprenticeships at the prestigious restaurants Guy Savoy and Maison Rostang.

After Lo returned to New York in 1991, she continued to hone her cooking style, first at Chanterelle and later as the executive chef at Mirezi. In 2000, she founded Annisa (Arabic for "women"), a contemporary American restaurant in New York City's West Village, where she applied classical French techniques to globally inspired flavors. After the restaurant suffered a devastating electrical fire in 2009, Lo traveled the world, exploring the cuisines of locations like Senegal, Alaska, and Russia, and later incorporated those influences into the menu when the restaurant reopened in 2010.

As the first woman guest chef to collaborate on a state dinner at the White House, in 2015, Lo prepared a four-course, Chinese-inspired meal for President and Mrs. Obama and Chinese president Xi Jinping and his wife, Peng Liyuan. She has also appeared in numerous films and television shows, including *Top Chef Masters* and *Iron Chef: America*. Since closing Annisa in 2017, Lo spends her time writing recipes and cookbooks and hosting culinary tours around the world.

ABOVE

Lo chopping garlic
and ginger in her
New York kitchen

"I like to eat diversely, and it does depend on
the day and season. But there are a few dishes
I return to again and again, such as my mother's
steamed fish with ginger and scallions and two
recipes from my cookbook *Solo*: the smoky
eggplant frittata and the chile verde."

Jess Thomson

Jess Thomson is a Seattle-based writer, recipe developer, and author.

Two days before Thanksgiving, our son, age nine, swore in front of us for the first time. We were guiding our broken Outback into the dried grass along Interstate 84 near Nampa, Idaho, twenty miles short of Boise, our destination. "SH*T, that was scary," he said. We couldn't argue. We'd just survived a speedy four-car collision that also involved good friends and their kids. My mother came and collected our son and our friends' two children, while the rest of us shivered on the dark median, wondering how we were all basically OK. Tow truck lights painted our faces orange.

It's an odd time of year to have your world shaken. Not that it ever feels normal when metal hits metal hits metal hits metal, and four cars' worth of humans come pouring out of their smoking vehicles, checking for life and fire. The next morning, as we rehashed the accident, it didn't feel right to think about roasting a turkey.

But Thanksgiving is the holiday that means turkey, and in my family, for many years it's meant me at the helm of a well-organized and overly ambitious cooking expedition. While in theory it has become my responsibility to cook

because I am the one with the most formal training, it's probably more accurate to say I cook because I'm the bossiest one. ("Force-feeder" is a moniker I've also heard.) I'm the one who makes the lists, guides the shopping carts, and freezes the piecrusts ahead of time.

The crash introduced a new sort of list to this Thanksgiving eve: Two families needed to tow cars to the correct body shops, call insurance agents, find rental cars, file police reports, and soothe worried relatives. Our friend had broken her collarbone and needed to get medical treatment. Losing control of the car also meant losing control of the holiday—of what got cooked where, when, and by whom. I wasn't sure how Thanksgiving could be Thanksgiving if I wasn't the one to make it be.

Instead, we focused on a pre-organized junk show we called the Thanksgiving Olympics. The first event was a pumpkin pie contest, which my grandmother would judge. Teams of two had to use my premade pie dough (which survived the crash), an intentionally flimsy paper pie plate, and the recipe from the back of a can of cooked pumpkin. The catch: One person had to be blindfolded, and that person had to make the pie, while the second person simply gave instructions. Moments after I started the timer—points would be awarded for speed, as well as for flavor and presentation—we traded in our trauma for hysteria as family and friends pawed through my poor mother's kitchen, flinging pumpkin and nutmeg near bowls but not always in them and rolling pie dough into awkward, jagged slabs. It was the equivalent of a group trust fall, an exercise unintentionally appropriate, considering the unexpectedness of our travel misadventure. The pies turned out looking more or less like pies. Morale improved. We didn't need me to make a perfect pie; we needed all of us to make imperfect pies together.

And when my sister churned out a spicy chicken wing–inspired gravy, I realized something had changed: I wasn't interested in making a flawless feast. I was reveling in the imperfection of the holiday because we were all alive to enjoy it. And unlike every previous Thanksgiving I'd cooked, when it came time to eat, I was actually starving.

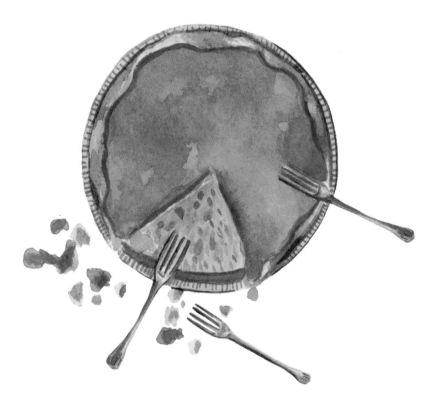

"I don't really think of cooking in terms of failure or success; it's just a process and an experience. At the end, you're different than when you began; you've grown or learned. But not because you've failed or succeeded."

—Irene Li
chef and owner of Mei Mei Restaurant

What do you think of as comforting or healing food?

"My ultimate comfort food is Chinese-style rice porridge. I like it totally plain or dressed up with all kinds of toppings."

—Irene Li
chef and owner of Mei Mei Restaurant
Boston, MA

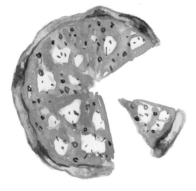

"There's a difference between comfort food and healing food, and both are important. When I think of comfort food, my number one go-to is nachos. Also, pizza. When I think of healing food, I think of the food that I want to eat after I've been sick. Nothing bland, but simple, with few ingredients: a beautiful matzo ball soup with delicious, homemade chicken broth, or roast chicken with brown rice."

—Zoe Schor
chef and owner of Split-Rail
and co-owner of Dorothy
Chicago, IL

"Eating foods that are in season provides us with the nutrition our bodies need to feel our best during that season. I think a diet that relies heavily on properly cooked vegetables with healing aromatics (ginger, turmeric, spices) and some humanely raised meat and that is void of processed food makes us feel better. Food cooked with intention and love is healing."

—Cheetie Kumar
chef and owner of Garland, Neptunes Parlour,
and Kings and rock guitarist
Raleigh, NC

"Comfort food, for me, is absolutely the dishes from my childhood. My mother, an Italian immigrant, cooked food made from scratch every night. Now, as an adult, I truly appreciate the effort she put into our meals. So whenever I need a pick-me-up, I visit my mom. I lift the lid of the pot that seems to be always simmering on the stove, and I am transported right back to my younger self and to simpler days."

—Anna Francese Gass
chef, recipe tester, and food writer
New York, NY

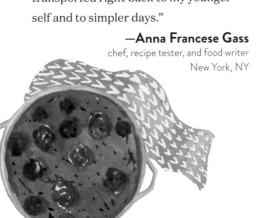

"Soups and braises. There is something about the long, slow simmer and the amazing, comforting flavor-building that make me feel instantly relaxed and healed. There is nothing better than sitting around the dinner table with my family with a piping hot bowl of homemade soup and cornbread."

—Katie Button
executive chef and CEO of
Katie Button Restaurants
Asheville, NC

"Food that I know deeply. Once it was a glass of California Chalone wine that told me I was home during a time when I was struggling with being back in the US."

—Deborah Madison
chef, cooking teacher,
master gardener, and author
Galisteo, NM

Katianna Hong

After graduating from the Culinary Institute of America in 2005, chef Katianna Hong worked her way up through some of the most competitive kitchens in the country. In 2009, she moved from Los Angeles to Northern California to work as a line cook at the Restaurant at Meadowood in Napa, where, in 2014, she became the only woman chef de cuisine at a three-star Michelin restaurant in the United States. Later, she helped open the nearby Charter Oak Restaurant, where she was the chef for three years.

While Hong's success and creative freedom were exhilarating, the demands of the job were also unrelenting. She and her husband, chef John Hong, wanted kids, and she began to question the personal sacrifices she felt she had to make to maintain her edge in the restaurant world. In 2019, Hong got pregnant and worked at Charter Oak through the eighth month of her pregnancy before stepping down. After their daughter's birth, Hong and her husband relocated to Los Angeles to be closer to relatives and pursue a professional life that incorporates their family and Korean heritage.

Breakfast in Anyang

Food has been instrumental in identifying with my culture. I am an adopted Korean American who came to the United States when I was only three months old. I grew up in upstate New York and, despite the best efforts of my parents, had limited access to Korean cultural experiences. At a certain age, I developed an intense curiosity about where I came from and who had made me. I tried without success to find my birth mother. I also tried to engage in Korean culture. My mother would drive me to a small Korean market a half hour away and I would roam the aisles and explore for what seemed like hours. I had never seen so many Asian food products in one place. It was a whole new world compared to the half of an aisle dedicated to "ethnic" products at our local market. Who knew there was more

than one kind of soy sauce? And tofu with different degrees of firmness?

When I was fourteen, I went on my first trip to Korea. I visited temples, watched traditional Korean dancing, shopped in the street markets of Seoul, and ate anchovies for the first time. During my visit, I spoke to a woman on the street who, upon realizing that I didn't speak Korean, said to me, "Oh, you are not really Korean, you just look Korean." Her words hurt me and totally turned me off from further exploration of my culture.

It wasn't until I started dating John, my first-generation Korean American husband, that I dabbled with the idea of exploring my roots again. We decided to eat our way through South Korea, starting in Seoul, traveling down the coast, and making our way to Jeju Island, which is famous for its oranges and pork. We even stopped at my birthplace in the countryside province of Chungcheongnam-do, where I first experienced the chewy joy of homemade knife-cut noodles.

LEFT
Miyeok guk served alongside rice, kimchee, jap chae, and pork belly at Hong's family gathering

We later went back to Korea for a family vacation, during which we had the opportunity to enjoy an elaborate Korean breakfast prepared by John's eighty-seven-year-old grandmother. When we arrived midmorning, she was scurrying around to set a traditional Korean table that sat close to the floor. Cushions were laid out for each of us. Upon removing our shoes, we took our seats on the floor and scooted up to the table.

The first thing I noticed were individual steamy bowls of pearly white rice. With rice almost always comes kimchee and a soup or stew (sometimes both). In this case, she served us a seaweed soup called miyeok guk. Its base was a light broth of beef and anchovy, studded with tiny shreds of beef tangled in a mass of tender green seaweed. The texture of the seaweed was soft yet had a bite. If you closed your eyes, you might have mistaken the seaweed for noodles. The surface of the soup was shimmering green with seaweed-infused droplets of beef fat. Although the soup consisted of only three ingredients, it was rich, smooth, and luxurious.

The jap chae (noodles made with sweet potato starch) were tossed with slices of marinated beef and an array of sautéed garlicky vegetables including red bell peppers, onions, carrots, and shiitake mushrooms. The noodles were perfectly seasoned with just a little toasty sesame oil, sesame seeds, and soy sauce.

She served three types of kimchee: one made of small whole ponytail radishes (chonggakmu); one young, "fresh" cabbage version; and one older, aged cabbage version. The younger was more peppery and sweet, while the older was more sour and complex.

The raw marinated crabs—salty, spicy, slightly sweet—were a favorite among the family. They had been cut into pieces before being marinated and lightly preserved in a sauce of rice wine, plum syrup, garlic, soy sauce, sesame seeds, and a ton of gochugaru, or Korean chili flakes. My favorite part of the meal was the boiled pork belly simmered just until tender and dipped in a sauce of salted shrimp, garlic, green onions, red pepper flakes, and sesame oil. John's grandmother kept apologizing that she had overcooked the pork, but I thought it was perfect.

I'd had these dishes many times before, but for some reason, on this morning, they were better. I'm not sure if that was due to his grandmother's cooking skills or just the fact that I was witnessing this older woman under five feet tall with silvery white hair slowly present the dishes she had spent all morning preparing. She refused to sit down and join us for the meal. Instead she stood watchfully, refilling empty dishes, offering more tea, and carefully maintaining the table. She doted on us with such care and concern.

Food has given me a feeling of cultural belonging and a long-desired sense of peace. This trip and the connection we felt inspired John and me to start our own family. Two months later, we found out I was pregnant, and in September 2019 we welcomed our first daughter. The miyeok guk soup that we had eaten at John's grandmother's home is also known as birthday soup. It is traditionally served to mothers who have just given birth to aid in healing and regaining strength, and the child is supposed to eat the soup every year on their birthday to honor their mother. I ate this soup every day for the first month after having my daughter, and every time it took me back to that special breakfast prepared with love by John's grandmother.

Bakers Who Give Back

How is your bakery involved in your community?

"Justice of the Pies considers itself to be a social mission in a culinary art form. Our community involvement ranges from collaborating with nonprofit organizations to raise money and awareness, to mentoring and overseeing workshops that teach kids from underserved communities basic kitchen skills with a focus on nutritional development. The primary goal of our youth workshops is to contribute to ending food insecurities. It's something I feel deeply about because I've seen how it affected my family and how the trauma of those experiences can be passed down. Eating well is the first step to living well, sleeping well, learning well, feeling well, being well."

—**Maya-Camille Broussard**
chef and owner of Justice of the Pies
Chicago, IL

"Baking is the way I communicate with people. After going to pastry school and working in kitchens in New York City, I learned to love the work even more and hoped to bring the experiences I had to Lincoln, Nebraska, the community I was from. To me, opening a bakery meant building a community around food.

"With a staff of mostly women, I learned really quickly how powerful positive relationships are among women and the rolling impact those relationships have as we create our lives. In 2018, I started Empower Through Flour, an annual campaign during Women's History Month that brings together women in the food industry to support I Am That Girl, a nonprofit organization that champions girls' empowerment."

—**Angela Garbacz**
pastry chef and owner of Goldenrod Pastries and
founder of Empower Through Flour
Lincoln, NE

"We connect to our community in various ways, including offering a discount to folks in our zip code and occasionally giving away free spots in our popular pie classes. My favorite way to connect, outside of daily interactions with regulars, is by asking for feedback. As we plan for an expansion, our neighbors have communicated their hopes and dreams in meetings and surveys. We're stronger because we're building Sister Pie's future together."

—**Lisa Ludwinski**
chef and owner of Sister Pie
Detroit, MI

"Every time we do a Gather For Good bake sale, it brings people out of their homes and into a local setting to engage with each other. Bake sales pull a community together and get neighbors who might otherwise pass each other in the street to start talking about all kinds of things, including how they can improve their world, starting with their neighborhoods and spreading out to local government and beyond."

—Laurel Almerinda
pastry chef and director of bakery operations
at Huckleberry Bakery & Café
Santa Monica, CA

What excites you most about going to work each day?

"Seeing joy and satisfaction on the faces of those who enjoy my pies, my classes and workshops, our collaborations, or my mentorship. The connections make the work worthwhile, and knowing that I'm walking in my true calling makes it gratifying."

—Maya-Camille Broussard
chef and owner of Justice of the Pies
Chicago, IL

"To see the family we have created through feeding ourselves, each other, and our customers is astounding. We are trusted to be a part of the most intimate moments in people's lives. I got into this field because I absolutely love making food, and I love giving that food to people and watching them enjoy it."

—Angela Garbacz
pastry chef and owner of Goldenrod Pastries and
founder of Empower Through Flour
Lincoln, NE

"My life really changed the day I became a boss. At Sister Pie we take care of each other, and we're defining what that means together. We spend so much of our lives at work, so trying to create goodness and value there gets me out of bed every day."

—Lisa Ludwinski
chef and owner of Sister Pie
Detroit, MI

"Working with other creative, dynamic, and powerful women. Seeing the amazing things they do on a daily basis. The huge last-minute catering orders they pull together with the utmost care. The love they put into everything they make."

—Laurel Almerinda
pastry chef and director of bakery operations
at Huckleberry Bakery & Café
Santa Monica, CA

Elizabeth Binder

CHEF ELIZABETH BINDER'S love of food and travel was ingrained from a very young age. Growing up amid apartheid in Durban, South Africa, she was influenced by her father, a British fisherman who loved to cook, and her maternal grandmother, who hosted weekly formal family dinners. Binder pored over cookbooks and magazines, clipping recipes for her red tartan recipe book and experimenting with whatever ingredients she could find. International sanctions meant that many ingredients were unavailable, but every few years, Granny England—as Binder called her—visited and brought with her a suitcase stuffed to the brim with homemade pasties, tinned fish, savoy cabbage, and other specialties. These much-anticipated treats were edible windows into Binder's heritage and the world beyond.

At her family's urging, Binder attended culinary school, and quickly afterward, at nineteen years old, she became head chef of Blue Mountain Lodge, where where she cooked state dinners for President F. W. de Klerk and his successor, Nelson Mandela, during a pivotal period in South African history.

Later, she traveled across the world to work in fine kitchens in England, France, and Australia. She finally landed in San Francisco, where she became the partner and executive chef of the much-loved Bar Bambino. In 2012, Elizabeth founded Hand-Crafted Catering, a boutique catering company in Napa Valley, where she specializes in rustically elegant food, sustainably sourced from local farms and her own garden.

BELOW

Binder's polenta cake served on dishes she inherited from her mother, aunt, and grandmother

Citrus Almond Polenta Cake

Serves 8 or more

I am often asked for the recipe for this unforgettable cake. I first put this on the menu at Bar Bambino, where it was an instant success. It has the most amazing honey notes, which come from the combination of the citrus, almond, and polenta, and is decidedly delicious. Sticky sweet and crumbly, moist on the inside and crusty on the outside. Fabulous served for dessert (or even breakfast) alongside an espresso.

❶ Preheat the oven to 300°F. Grease a 9-inch springform cake tin with butter, and line the bottom with parchment paper.

❷ Beat the eggs, yolks, and sugar in a large bowl until pale and fluffy. Fold in the almond meal, polenta, and baking powder. Add the citrus zest and juice to the cake batter and mix well to thoroughly combine.

❸ Pour the cake batter into the cake tin and place in the center of the oven. Bake for 1 hour and 15 minutes before checking with a skewer. The top should have a firm crust and the inside should be moist but not wet. Cook for additional time as needed (be patient—this cake sometimes needs more time than expected). Remove from the oven and cool in the tin.

❹ Dust the cake with confectioners' sugar and serve with whipped mascarpone.

Butter, for greasing the pan

5 large eggs

2 egg yolks from large eggs

1 pound plus 4 ounces granulated sugar

1 pound almond meal

1½ ounces polenta

1 teaspoon baking powder

Zest and juice of 1 orange, 1 lemon, and 1 lime (use a Microplane)

Confectioners' sugar, for serving

Mascarpone cheese, for serving

IN CONVERSATION

Describe a cooking failure or success and how it impacted you.

"I was fired from my first professional baking job after working for only a month. Part of my job was to make the restaurant's signature chocolate cake, which included almonds, raisins, and whiskey. After a few weeks, I got bored, and so without telling anyone, I changed the recipe— I made it with pecans, prunes, and Armagnac. That afternoon I was fired for 'creative insubordination.' At the time I was devastated, but years later I saw it as a triumph. I also saw it as the beginning of my career creating recipes and started putting sections in my books called 'Playing Around,' which give permission to other cooks and bakers to try a little creative insubordination."

—Dorie Greenspan
writer, *New York Times Magazine*
columnist, and author
New York, NY, and Paris, France

"I remember the first time I left my restaurant in the hands of another chef. Walking back into the dining room and hearing a guest tell me how much they loved a dish (that was not mine) felt amazing. It is really a team effort, and feeling that love in response to all of us working together is the best."

—Renee Erickson
chef and co-owner of
Sea Creatures restaurants
Seattle, WA

"I don't really think of cooking in terms of failure or success; it's just a process and an experience. At the end, you're different than when you began; you've grown or learned. But not because you've failed or succeeded."

—Irene Li
chef and owner of *Mei Mei Restaurant*
Boston, MA

"A few years ago, I had the opportunity to prepare the dessert course for Spanish chef Albert Adrià and his Hoja Santa team. I baked chocolate chip cookies—I always crave chocolate under stress! Chef Adrià ate one after another and eventually asked me for the recipe. I thought he was only being polite, but I received an email the next day from his chef de cuisine requesting the recipe. It was an amazing day: To be acknowledged as a young cook who made something simple but out of love was an incredible feeling.

"As for cooking failures, these happen all the time! You experience them on a daily basis, but they are what make you a better cook and person. You need the downs to cherish the ups."

—**Isabel Coss**
pastry chef at Cosme
New York, NY

Minara Begum & Emily Staugaitis

of Bandhu Gardens

MINARA BEGUM AND Emily Staugaitis first got to know each other when they became neighbors in Detroit, Michigan, a city that is home to one of the biggest Bangladeshi populations in the United States. Begum, her husband, and their children arrived from Bangladesh in 2015, and Begum's brother owned a house across the street, which he rented to Staugaitis. Planting the seeds she carried from home, Begum, who did not yet speak English, grew a lush garden and often sent her daughters to Staugaitis's house to invite her to join them for a meal. Food quickly became the neighbors' common language—they spent time together in Begum's kitchen and garden, pointing to objects and repeating the name in both English and Bangla.

As the women learned to communicate, their friendship grew. Staugaitis helped Begum navigate life in the United States, and Begum fed Staugaitis and shared her wealth of garden knowledge, which had been instilled in her as a young child. "I started learning in the garden with my mom and aunties when I was very little, three or four years old," Begum recalls.*

Over time, Staugaitis met other Bangladeshi women in the neighborhood through her friendship with Begum, and she noticed that they too kept vibrant backyard gardens with plants like winter squash, amaranth greens, and bitter melon, and many of them were searching for ways to offset their families' expenses. "It has been harder than I thought it would be [in the United States]. In Bangladesh we grew all of our own food, so we didn't need to buy as much. America is expensive!" Begum says. Simultaneously, Staugaitis became aware of a growing number of Detroit restaurants eager to source local produce and wondered if she could serve as a link between the two communities.

That's when Bandhu Gardens was born. She and Begum formed a network of Bangladeshi women who sold surplus produce from their gardens to local restaurants and farmers markets, creating extra income that helped provide for their families in Michigan or relatives in Bangladesh.

Now the organization, whose members range from five to seventy-six years old, also offers catering services and hosts cooking classes and pop-up dinners that showcase traditional Bangladeshi produce and cuisine. These initiatives have become avenues for cultural connection within the Detroit community, a ripple effect of Begum and Staugaitis's own sisterly bond. "We would not be where we are without the friendships in Detroit," Staugaitis says. "All of our success has been through partnerships, primarily with women who have made space for, included, and promoted us."

Bandhu Gardens is now in the process of converting a neighborhood building to a permanent culinary studio for activities and after-school and community programs, all centered around food. "The goal is always to expand economic opportunities, build social connections and civic engagement, and improve access to resources across our diverse community," Staugaitis says.

Bandhu, which means "friend" in Bangla, is an apt name for Begum and Staugaitis's partnership. Staugaitis sums up their approach with one of her favorite proverbs: "If you want to go fast, go alone. If you want to go far, go together."

*Quotes from Minara Begum were originally spoken in Bangla and translated to English by Emily Staugaitis.

"Food should not only feed the body, but the spirit of the entire community."

—Hillel Echo-Hawk
chef and owner of
Birch Basket Catering
and Indigenous food
sovereignty activist

"I am very proud of that restaurant. I'm proud of my writing. I'm proud of my family—I've got good kids. I was a single working parent. I'm proud that I did a lot of this on my own."

ABOVE

Goldstein at home in San Francisco, preparing to make jam with quince from the farmers market

Joyce Goldstein

JOYCE GOLDSTEIN IS a chef, prolific author, and restaurant consultant. Originally from Brooklyn, New York, Goldstein lived in Rome as a young woman and traveled extensively throughout the Mediterranean region, an experience that exposed her to global flavors and developed her acute "taste memory." After settling in the San Francisco Bay Area in 1960, Goldstein, who is a voracious learner and completely self-taught, founded the California Street Cooking School, San Francisco's first international cooking school, before becoming the chef of the café at Alice Waters's Chez Panisse.

In 1984, Goldstein opened her San Francisco–based restaurant, Square One, where she pioneered a menu that incorporated the foods of Italy, Spain, France, Greece, Turkey, the Middle East, and North Africa. In the kitchen, Goldstein was keenly invested in educating her staff on the food they made and served and encouraged experimentation. In the dining room, she viewed interactions with guests as a "wonderful partnership," actively seeking feedback to relay back to the kitchen. "I never realized it was unusual," she says. "That's how I did it—I taught myself and I taught them." The restaurant closed its doors in 1996, but she remains proud of the relationships she maintains with many of her staff to this day.

Goldstein says the highlights of her career include cooking many times for her culinary hero, English cookbook author and writer Elizabeth David, as well as for famed food writer MFK Fisher. Endlessly curious and ambitious, Goldstein keeps her cellar full of meticulously stacked homemade jams and preserves, made with fruit from the farmers market at San Francisco's Ferry Building, which she visits every week.

Christa Chase

ORIGINALLY FROM ARIZONA, chef Christa Chase got her start cooking at Black Angus Steakhouse during high school. After graduating from culinary school, she moved to Northern California in 2008, eager to immerse herself in the renowned local food scene. As a young chef, she cooked in some of Oakland's most esteemed restaurants under the mentorship of chefs like Paul Canales and Julia Shin, but she also endured the toxic masculinity and sexism that commonly prevail in restaurant kitchens.

In 2016, she was offered the position of executive chef at San Francisco's Tartine Manufactory, where she oversaw more than thirty chefs and porters and worked hard to establish a culture based on collaboration and open communication. A year later, amid the heightened political atmosphere following Donald Trump's election and the momentum of the #MeToo movement, Chase became inspired to use her platform and voice to advocate for women chefs' and workers' rights.

Ready for a change, Chase left Tartine to join Blake Sondel Cole and Kimberly Rosselle in building a bar in Oakland from the ground up. The trio envisioned an open-minded, inviting space, owned by an all-women team with a clear set of operating values. "Being back in Oakland and working alongside a group of women who I respected for their vision and values was worth the leap," she says. In 2020, Friends and Family opened in Oakland's Uptown neighborhood, with Chase as chef.

The chance to develop a menu for the intimate setting and engage with a small staff was a notable but appealing change from her previous role. At Friends and Family, her team of six cooks covers the full range of tasks (including dishwashing) in a kitchen limited to induction burners and an under-counter oven. She enjoys the challenge of these constraints and

ABOVE

Chase's halibut crudo with marsh grapefruit, chia seeds in green juice, puffed quinoa, and lime and fish sauce vinaigrette. "Being from Arizona and not having local seafood available, I was so excited when I moved here and [was] amazed by everything that lives in our oceans," she says.

As a team, Sondel Cole, Rosselle, and Chase foster a work environment that prizes respect, honest communication, and opportunities for learning and growth. "Collaboration challenges you to be vulnerable to other people's criticisms, to leave your ego behind and be open to having a discussion about what makes something better. I don't think that one person is the holder of all the great ideas," Chase says.

This venture also allowed her the freedom to expand her activism efforts. In 2019, she cofounded Bay Area Fight for Abortion Rights, a campaign that enlisted eighty restaurants and bars to raise money for Planned Parenthood and resulted in a $40,000 donation. Since then, Chase and her cofounders have coordinated multiple community-building events, including A Day of Give & Take, a fundraiser hosted by Friends and Family on International Women's Day in 2020. "I am excited every day to be supported by this community and have the opportunity to do this work with such an amazing group of women," Chase says.

pushes herself and her team to play with new ideas that fit the space. The menu, which focuses on shared plates, includes "Potato Things," a riff on classic potato latkes and a nod to Sondel Cole's Jewish heritage; vegan roasted broccolini with black sesame vinaigrette; and an ever-changing take on crudo, one of Chase's favorite blank canvases for experimentation.

What season makes you most excited to cook?

Spring: 7%

"It's the first time fresh produce is available after the winter. I always look forward to asparagus, peas, and ramps."

—Rebecca
Brooklyn, NY

"I love all of the spring herbs that pop up, like thyme, mint, rosemary, cilantro, basil, and parsley. I also really enjoy sorrel because it has a very unique lemon flavor and is a wonderful addition to a salad with a bright vinaigrette."

—Heather
Gulf Breeze, FL

"I love the abundance of spring and the leeks and all the greens."

—Cara
Vienna, VA

"In late spring (May), I love making goodies with strawberries."

—Julia
Richmond, VA

Summer: 27%

"It's more about the experience than the food itself, although I do love salads with fresh nectarines and grilled corn on the cob. I associate summer with late nights, eating outside, enjoying a glass of wine, and feeling less rushed in general. There's something lighter about that time of year."

—Chantal
Oakland, CA

"I subscribe to a CSA [community-supported agriculture] and look forward to farm-fresh veggies and fruit that I otherwise might not buy, like garlic scapes and kohlrabi."

—Alice
Pittsburgh, PA

"I love to cook on the grill, and although I use it year-round, it's so much easier when it's warm outside and still light. It's great to use for broccoli, eggplant, and zucchinis."

—Shannon
Rye, NY

"Tomatoes, stone fruit—everything is so ripe and juicy! I love to find recipes that play with tanginess, sweetness, and freshness."

—Linnea
Los Angeles, CA

Fall: 42%

"I love to cook slow dishes—stews and one-pots. I think potatoes are just great. And there are lots of autumnal excuses for melty cheese."

—Jeannelle
Rockville, MD

"Fall is cozy. Produce in New England is still great (squash, greens) and the apple orchards call."

—Alexandra
Andover, MA

"Cool weather is perfect for warm dishes and soups and stews. Love eggplant, brussels sprouts, fall pears, and plums."

—Diane
Grand Rapids, MI

"Moose season! Berry season! Mushroom season!"

—Andi
Kenai, AK

Winter: 24%

"Winter holidays, from Christmas and Lunar New Year to the Scottish Burns supper, the Super Bowl, and Valentine's Day, allow me to be creative and festive."

—Edna
Missouri City, TX

"Hearty soups and stews, curries, fresh bread, cookies, pies—they warm the house and the spirit. I love summer produce, but cooking is less fun for me because it's hot and I'd rather be playing outside."

—Regina
Williamstown, MA

"I love to cook in the winter because winters are so long up here. I make lots of homemade chili, chicken noodle soup, shrimp alfredos, and beef stews."

—Hallie
Wasilla, AK

"Because in the winter you want to curl up with hot, homemade meals! I use lots of herbs (picked from my garden in the summer and frozen), carrots, leeks, and potatoes."

—Catie
Woodstock, VT

ESSAY BY

Osayi Endolyn

Osayi Endolyn is a Brooklyn-based writer and author whose award-winning work focuses on food and identity.

Like Paradise

The blue-brown kitchen on Hazeltine Avenue is the one I loved the most. Quirkier than the white facades that sparkled in my childhood homes or the bland ones that would come later, the blue-brown kitchen sold me on my first solo apartment. A family friend helped me find a one-bedroom, third-floor walk-up north of the canyon in Sherman Oaks, a neighborhood in Los Angeles. The Shangri-La was not utopia, but the rectangular building that bordered a pristine pool was quiet and cozy.

My last living situation had unfolded right before my eyes. A naive college sophomore, I'd prematurely left the dorms and moved in with a junior who happened to pledge a historically Black sorority around the same time. Back then, printed photos wrapped in drugstore packaging could lie about unattended: On the subject of that chapter's initiation rituals involving hacked-off hair, tear-streaked faces, and food-stained walls, I still have many questions. My roommate's "sisters" treated our apartment like their own. One night a woman I didn't like was surfing the web in my room on my new, blue iMac. Some nights a chorus of moans cascaded down the hall. (The internet tells me my roomie and her boyfriend headed to Spain and had four kids. They had plenty of practice.) When moving time came, someone took off with my computer. But my new place, the whole space—it was mine.

The Shangri-La was generic, save for my kitchen and bathroom. Both were bedecked with small squares of vintage Los Angeles tile. In the bathroom, they were seafoam green

to contrast with the bright pink sink and the bright pink bathtub. Once, my constantly pregnant building super, who was Mormon and had Joni Mitchell hair, came up to investigate a clogged sink. I didn't expect that she'd pull back the frosted glass shower door to see if the tub was also having issues. She came face-to-face with my bright pink waterproof dildo, which I'd forgotten to remove from the soap dish. "It's a perfect match!" I offered to her scowling glare.

In my tiny kitchen, the countertop and backsplash tile were a rich navy blue, which offset the dark, decades-old gas range with the shiny brown oven with the pilot light that was always snuffed out. My wood cabinets were almost always bare. Most days I ate elsewhere, a result of commuting across town to Westwood, Culver City, Marina del Rey, or Beverly Hills, depending on the day. I owned one royal-blue four-piece dining set from Ikea. I had one skillet, one pot, one pair of oven mitts. Trader Joe's across the street was my go-to for flour tortillas, avocado, a container of spicy red salsa, and a small block of Jack cheese. I owned no cookbooks. I didn't entertain. I was alone. And it was fabulous.

I'd make my one quesadilla with the precision of a wedding cake artisan. Carefully, I sliced thin rectangles of cheese, layered them across a tortilla fried to just-crisp. With my One Good Knife I'd slice the oozing circle in half, then into quarters, and then I'd place it alongside halved avocados with a dollop of salsa. Often, I ate standing up in the kitchen. Sometimes, I sat cross-legged on my sofa and watched TV. Maybe I'd rinse the plate before going to bed for the night. Usually, I'd leave it for the morning.

"The beautiful thing about cooking is, there's always tomorrow. . . . Nobody is born knowing how to be a great chef— it's all through practice and hard work."

—Samin Nosrat
chef, writer, and television host

Liz Alpern

LIZ ALPERN'S DESIRE to explore identity and bring people together through food has always been at the core of her entrepreneurial spirit. She says it all began when she was a college student, living on her own and often hosting friends for home-cooked meals, Jewish holidays, and Friday Shabbat. She loved every aspect of these gatherings: the preparation and planning, cooking and hosting, sharing food and stories. She even tinkered with her recipe for challah until it was so good that she sold it from her apartment, soaking up the simple pleasure of every exchange.

After college, she worked at one of New York City's oldest vegetarian restaurants, Angelica Kitchen, where she encountered new foods and learned about seasonality, a concept that had not yet become mainstream. She considered going to culinary school, but she wound up working for legendary cookbook author and Jewish food expert Joan Nathan instead. A number of exploratory culinary jobs followed, but her love of Jewish food never faded.

In 2009, she met her business partner, Jeffrey Yoskowitz, who shared her concern that Eastern European Jewish food was on the precipice of extinction, and they decided to do something about it. That same year, they cofounded the Gefilteria, a food venture that reimagines old-world Jewish foods. Their first creation was a signature artisanal gefilte fish, a sustainably sourced and high-quality revival of a classic Ashkenazi dish that most people had only eaten out of a jar. They now sell the seasonal product online and in stores along the East Coast in addition to teaching classes and workshops on Jewish food, history, and culture and hosting educational pop-up dinners all over the country.

After Donald Trump's victory in the 2016 presidential election, an especially unsettling and dark time for the LGBTQ+ community, Alpern

"Even when I was a kid, I loved soup, and it has always been my favorite food."

felt called to political action. She was searching for a way to contribute to the resistance, and she had always dreamed of hosting a queer soup party. It seemed like the perfect time to fuse her ideas: "Soup is the comfort food of every culture, the food you have when you're sick, when someone wants to make you something nourishing," she says. The community was desperate for nourishment; she would give the people soup!

And so Queer Soup Night, a welcoming and inclusive party that features food by queer chefs and raises money for the resistance, was born. The first event was hosted in a bar in Brooklyn, New York, and attended mostly by Alpern's friends. Since then, Queer Soup Night has multiplied to sixteen chapters around the country and has raised thousands of dollars to support local organizations working on issues important to the LGBTQ+ community, including mental health, food justice, and prison reform.

> "I really care about queer people feeling queer—loving our queer selves and being happy to be queer—because I think that we are better additions to society when that is true."

Each party draws hundreds of people, queer and non-queer, who are welcomed warmly at the door. "Being greeted is part of feeling nourished and safe," Alpern says. "When you are met with a smile and a warm word, it's a sign that you can be your full queer self in this place, while enjoying chef-quality food and supporting a social justice organization. I try to send these kinds of messages in all the work that I do. As I'm greeting you with intention, I'm letting you know that you belong here."

Mimi Mendoza

PASTRY CHEF Mimi Mendoza never intended to be a chef. She originally pursued degrees in art and creative writing in San Francisco, but she often missed class, lured by her culinary experiments and the city's enticing food. Eventually she enrolled in culinary school and discovered her passion for pastry. After working for several acclaimed Bay Area restaurants, Mendoza was offered the position of opening pastry chef at the restaurant Senia in Honolulu. She saw the opportunity as a once-in-a-lifetime chance to connect with her roots: Her great-grandfather had immigrated there from the Philippines decades earlier, and she had spent summers there throughout her childhood.

At Senia, Mendoza's creations shine a spotlight on Hawaii's natural flavors and those of her heritage. Hibiscus, yuzu, tonka beans, and ube, a bright purple sweet potato common in Filipino cooking, infuse her colorful dishes. "I've always felt rooted here, like it [is] home for me," she says of Hawaii. "The ingredients available here are culturally close to my heart. Had I grown up in my great-grandparents' native Philippines, these are the ingredients I would have grown up loving."

Canelés de Bordeaux

Makes 12 canelés

When I was a young pastry cook in a French bistro, I worked for a short, scruffy pastry chef named Brian. He seemed to be angry all the time, but for some reason he invested in me. So whenever he expressed any sort of interest in something I made, I would get excited because it meant this "thing" would be amazing. One time around, it was a small, unassuming pastry called canelé de Bordeaux. Years later, I became the pastry chef at a restaurant where he had previously worked. I started practicing my canelé recipe there and it brought back so many good memories of learning from Chef Brian. To this day, I don't bake a single batch without thinking about him.

Note: Plan to make the batter at least 24 hours and preferably 48 hours in advance. The batter works best when it is allowed to sit overnight and mature.

❶ Sift the flour and confectioners' sugar together in a large bowl, then add the fleur de sel. In a separate bowl, whisk the whole eggs and the egg yolk together.

❷ Place the milk, browned butter, rum, vanilla beans, and tonka bean in a small pot and bring just to a boil over medium-high heat. Turn off the heat and ladle the liquid slowly into the egg mixture until homogenous. Using a whisk, slowly add the wet ingredients to the dry ingredients. Whisk just to incorporate—do not add air to the mixture! Allow the cooled mixture to sit in an airtight container in the fridge for a minimum of 24 hours before baking.

10 ounces all-purpose flour

1 pound plus 9 ounces confectioners' sugar

2 teaspoons fleur de sel

3 large eggs plus 1 large egg yolk

1½ quarts whole milk

5 ounces browned butter, strained

6 ounces Myers's rum

2 Tahitian vanilla beans

½ tonka bean (very powerful flavor)

8 ounces clarified butter

8 ounces pure beeswax

❸ When ready to bake, preheat the oven to 400°F. Combine the clarified butter and beeswax in a small pot and heat over high until the mixture is completely melted. The mixture is extremely hot—proceed with caution. Line 12 copper canelé molds (2½ inches in diameter) with the butter mixture. Fill each mold with batter to ¼ inch from the rim. Bake for 40 to 45 minutes, until the edges are evenly and deeply browned and butter is no longer pooled in the center.

❹ Place a cooling rack on top of a foil-lined baking sheet. Remove the canelés from the molds and place them on the rack to allow excess butter and beeswax to drip off. (The canelés will be soft when they first come out of the oven, but once they have cooled, the outer crusts will be crisp and hard.) Serve at room temperature within 8 hours of baking, to ensure that the exterior crusts are enjoyed when crispy and crunchy.

> "My intention is always flavor, but my process always starts out visually. Almost 100 percent [of the time] the food evolves from the idea in my head."

BELOW

Mendoza's canelés in a range of flavors (from left to right: classic, matcha, ube, churro, coffee)

Anya Fernald

ANYA FERNALD HAS dedicated her life to developing sustainable food practices—a journey inspired by being born on a cow dairy in Germany, where her parents, American professors, were teaching and doing research. When she was three, her family moved back to the United States and settled in Oregon, and later California, where she spent the rest of her childhood.

In her twenties, Fernald worked with small-scale food producers and farmers in Italy and other countries to create sustainable business models. She returned to California in 2006 and a year later became the executive director of Slow Food Nation, a four-day festival in San Francisco celebrating sustainable food with a local farmers market, an urban garden, music, workshops, speakers, films, and dinners highlighting the connection between food and nature.

But Fernald's exposure abroad to artisanal meats and cheeses made with low-intervention methods had left her longing for alternatives to the processed food products coming from the gigantic farm operations prevalent in the United States. She began buying meat directly from local producers and launched a small distribution company that sold nose-to-tail cuts of meat through a community-supported agriculture (CSA) group. These experiences confirmed what Fernald already knew: There was a need for sustainably farmed meat—and the subsequent health benefits—on a much bigger scale.

In 2012, she cofounded Belcampo Meat Co. with a mission to create a large-scale alternative meat supply system using regenerative and biodiverse farming methods that curb carbon emissions and revitalize and protect soils and watersheds.

RIGHT

Fernald in Belcampo's slaughterhouse, which was designed by animal-welfare expert Temple Grandin to ensure humane treatment of the animals in the facility

"I love the smell of dry-aging beef, so this room is one of my favorite places on earth."

At the base of California's Mount Shasta, Belcampo's cattle, chickens, pigs, ducks, and other livestock roam free on 25,000 acres of farmland and eat only grass before they are carefully butchered by hand in the company's slaughterhouse and sold online and in Belcampo's butcher shops and restaurants in California.

Contributors

What is your favorite ingredient?

"Flour! As a baker, I need to be able to create dough on a moment's notice."

—Reem Assil
chef and owner of Reem's California, entrepreneur, and activist
Oakland and San Francisco, CA

"Tie between cumin and coriander."

—Cheetie Kumar
chef and owner of Garland, Neptunes Parlour, and Kings and rock guitarist
Raleigh, NC

"Lemons, lemons, lemons! I love lemons. I love a good pucker."

—Carla Hall
chef, television personality, and author
Washington, DC

"I am never without a nice finishing vinegar. Acid plays a large role in my seasoning and I love something round and nutty, like Banyuls or Pedro Ximénez sherry vinegar. Just a dash on a grilled vegetable or a bowl of grains goes a long way."

—Caroline Glover
chef and founder of Annette
Aurora, CO

"Salt. I know this is kind of a gimme, but I think it's important to keep good kosher salt (not iodized table salt) in your home. I also highly recommend having a good flaky finishing sea salt on hand—Maldon and Falksalt are good brands."

—Zoe Schor
chef and owner of Split-Rail
and co-owner of Dorothy
Chicago, IL

"My mother's tomato sauce. She makes it in large batches and gives some to me so I can have one in the fridge and a few quart containers in my freezer at all times. It's liquid gold."

—Anna Francese Gass
chef, recipe tester,
and food writer
New York, NY

"Sesame seeds, specifically from Japan. The golden sesame seeds are the most delicious thing in the entire world. And vinegars from Katz, a farm based in Napa."

—Christa Chase
chef at
Friends and Family
Oakland, CA

Kate Williams

AFTER ATTENDING CULINARY school in France, Kate Williams traveled the globe for years, cooking at renowned restaurants in Chicago, New York, and Copenhagen. Eventually, she began to feel burned out from working in the high-stress environments and started questioning the meaning of her work. In 2014, she returned to her hometown of Detroit for a funeral, and the trip triggered a desire to reconnect with her multigenerational roots.

Williams grew up in a large Irish Catholic family, and her childhood memory reel always freezes on moments at the dining table, laughing and getting in trouble with her three brothers. "Food was a symbol for taking care of someone, taking care of your family. It was always about being together," she recalls. Inspiration returned in the form of a new dream: to own a restaurant that would be as

welcoming as the dining room of her childhood home and where she could cook every night.

In 2017, she opened her first restaurant in a former pub in Detroit's Corktown, the Irish neighborhood where her grandparents met decades earlier. To Williams, the restaurant's name, Lady of the House, is about reclaiming control—a symbol of power and grace, rather than domestic confinement. "Women have been running the show, we just haven't taken the credit for it. And now it's time," Williams says.

The space envelops diners in an atmosphere full of warmth and family history. When preparing to open, Williams came across boxes of china that her mother and grandmother had saved for her. The dishes felt symbolic: "They were setting me up to nurture and host others at my dinner table," she says. She put the vintage dishes

into rotation once the kitchen opened, and they quickly became the restaurant's trademark. Soon, guests started giving Williams their own long-forgotten family china to incorporate into Lady of the House's collection of past generations' plates, teacups, and saucers, all given new life.

The intersection of home and history is where Williams continues to find creative energy. In 2019, she opened another restaurant, Karl's, which has the vibe of a 1950s luncheonette. Named after A. Karl's Kercheval Home Bakery, which her great-great-grandparents ran on Detroit's east side, the new Karl's is Williams's projection of what the family business might have been if it hadn't closed after the Great Depression. Its classic menu is informed by her interviews with family members who shared stories and recipes, and family photos and memorabilia adorn the walls.

Though her vision is inspired by the past, Williams's cooking and leadership style are hallmarks of the contemporary moment. She prides herself on her nose-to-tail butchering in a no-waste kitchen, and she partners exclusively with local farms to supply the restaurant's meat and produce. As for the staff, everyone is given the opportunity to learn and advance, no matter their position or background. Williams considers every member of her team an important part of the restaurant's evolving story, and she proudly displays the childhood photos of current and past staff on the walls near the kitchen to send a message: *We're all in this together.*

The same integrity and intention are layered into the menu at Lady of the House. "Our most popular dishes, and the ones that I feel most connected to, are very simple and humble," Williams says. A prime example is her Parisian ham plate: ham from a local farm that has been butchered in-house, brined for two weeks, and slow-cooked with painstaking precision. The meat is shaved thin—bold, lovely pink-marbled ribbons with nothing to hide—and layered beside a dish of fermented local honey and Dijon butter. "We've found our success and our voice by just being true to what our food is," she says.

Lady of the House on Bagley Street in Detroit's historic Corktown neighborhood

"I'm not serving a menu, I'm serving a story. I'm serving my soul."

—Dominique Crenn
chef, restaurateur, and author

What obstacles have you overcome to get where you are today, and what have those experiences taught you about perseverance?

"I've had a lot of loss in my life. My goals and perseverance come from wanting to make my family and myself proud. This work is a marathon, not a sprint. It is also not for the faint of heart."

—**Julia Coney**
wine writer, educator, consultant,
and founder of Black Wine Professionals
Washington, DC, and Houston, TX

"Having our voices heard was and is still an obstacle. When trying to break into the industry, we were told that our ideas wouldn't work or be successful. And even after being in the industry for more than fifteen years, we experience other industry members doubting our wine knowledge and qualifications. But tenacity pays off, and perseverance taught us that sometimes it just takes one person to believe in us, because they'll carry our voice for us."

—**Robin McBride** (president) **&
Andréa McBride John** (CEO)
cofounders of McBride Sisters Wine Collection
Oakland, CA

"One obstacle that I struggle with daily is remembering to carve out a little bit of time for myself and that I have to be healthy in order to be the engine of the entire team. I think I'm getting better and better at it every day, but I've realized it's something that you have to work on and make a priority.

"When it comes to perseverance, you just have to keep going and working every day. I'm extremely optimistic, which is also one of my weaknesses because a lot of the time that can be challenging for the team, but I feel that it always works out in the end. One of my mottos is 'Don't freak out—always try to not freak out.'"

—**Jen Pelka**
cofounder of Une Femme Wines
San Francisco, CA, and New York, NY

"As one of the few women winery presidents, and consequently usually the only woman in high-level meetings, I had to learn to navigate carefully to avoid being either run over by being too nice or labeled a bitch by being too aggressive. I learned to be both gracious and ruthless. I knew I was setting a precedent for other women and was determined to prove women's ability. I had to prove to myself, as well as others, that I could do it."

—Susan Sokol Blosser
founder of Sokol Blosser Winery and author
Dayton, OR

"In Europe, particularly Portugal, Spain, Italy, and France, unless your family owns a vineyard or a winery, it's very difficult to thrive as a woman in the wine industry. At times I felt I had to work twice as hard as my male peers in order to prove myself. I had to move to another country. I had to overcome being a woman [in the industry] and being an immigrant. But I always knew what I wanted, I knew I had the talent. And every time something got in my way, I said to hell with it—I can do it and I'm going to show them I can do it."

—Ana Diogo-Draper
director of winemaking at
Artesa Vineyards & Winery
Napa, CA

"I grew up in a very small fishing town in the Philippines. I didn't know my mom until I was four years old because she worked in the US to send money to my family for my well-being. When my father died, she brought me to the US, and I had to learn a new language and a new way of life. That ended up being amazing for me, because it gave me a higher level of equity that allowed my hard work to mean something. I am a woman business owner of multiple restaurants and a master sommelier. There are not a lot of those around. I wish there were more.

"Lots of my skills came by sheer necessity—if I did not learn how to speak English, I would not be able to speak to anyone. I had to be very aware of my surroundings and became extremely intuitive because sometimes language and culture did not translate to the person I was trying to speak to. I still use that intuition today and try to speak to people in many different ways. Just like all paths are different, people translate words, phrases, body language, everything differently. It's important to be open-minded and intuitive at the same time."

—June Rodil
master sommelier and partner at
Goodnight Hospitality and June's All Day
Houston, TX

"I decided to walk away from a partnership (with two male partners) when one of them asked me to sign a clause stating that I would surrender my equity if I got pregnant within the first two years. While the decision was difficult, it led to a strong sense of conviction about my value system. That, in turn, ultimately led me to create Ramona [wine coolers]. Perseverance is everything! When you have a dream, fight for it."

—**Jordan Salcito**
sommelier, founder of
Ramona and Bellus Wines, and
director of Wine Special Projects
at Momofuku
New York, NY

"My greatest obstacle has always been my health: both mental and physical issues that I deal with, even now, on a near daily basis. Writing a book has been very positive for me. It's turned my health problems from obstacles working against my success to building blocks for my success. I no longer look at myself as having persevered despite my health problems, but rather, I have persevered because of them. It's not always easy, but I know they contribute to my unique talent and offerings."

—**Jane Lopes**
sommelier and cofounder of
LEGEND Wine Imports
Los Angeles, CA

"Everyone has obstacles; everyone has shit in their way and baggage behind them and personality flaws and weaknesses and fears. You either become a victim and let those circumstances become excuses, or you get back up again and again and again and again and say 'Yes, AND.' Yes, that just happened, and I am still going to do this. Yes, this is a massive struggle, and I can still try again. Yes, these emotions and anxieties feel like too much, and I won't stop. What I've learned about perseverance is you just Do the Damn Thing."

—**Stevie Stacionis**
sommelier, co-owner of
MAMA Oakland and Bay Grape,
and founder of Bâtonnage Forum
Oakland, CA

Arielle Johnson

Scientist Arielle Johnson is deeply curious about why and how we taste and perceive flavor. After earning her BS in chemistry from New York University and her PhD in flavor chemistry and gastronomy from University of California, Davis, Johnson landed in Copenhagen, Denmark. There she cofounded the Fermentation Lab at chef René Redzepi's restaurant, Noma, and became the head of research at MAD (Danish for "food"), Redzepi's food symposium and think tank.

She is now the science officer for Alton Brown's television show Good Eats *on the Food Network and frequently collaborates with chefs, restaurants, and bars around the world on creative projects, education, and flavor development. Her writing on food, flavor, science, and culture has appeared in* Lucky Peach, *the* Los Angeles Times, *and* Mold *magazine.*

Flavor: The Science You Vibe with

Flavor is a sensation, a sensory system, and an interpretation of specific molecules. Let's look at a strawberry as an example. The flavor we perceive happens when specific molecules from the strawberry bind to sensory receptors in our noses and mouths, which send a signal to our brains, where it is processed and interpreted.

When experiencing the flavor of a strawberry, you might notice that it tastes good. (That is, if you like strawberries. Maybe you don't like strawberries and they taste bad to you. But they almost certainly taste bad in a specific way, so read on.) Go a bit deeper and analyze and name your sensations—you'll notice that it's sweet, a little sour, fruity, jammy, floral, slightly green or grassy, and a bit caramelized. But the strawberry has no flowers in it, no grass, and it's not actually caramelized; it's a fruit. So where do those flavors come from? We need to look at the molecules that make a strawberry taste like strawberry. There are sugar molecules and acid molecules that account for the sweet and sour, but there's also a fruity-smelling molecule called ethyl hexanoate, which shows up in bananas and pineapples, too. There's another one called linalool, which smells floral and sweet and is found in lots of flowers, like elderflower and lavender. Trans-2-hexenal lends a grassy note and is an important component in the bouquet of cut grass. Finally, strawberries naturally make a molecule called furaneol, which has a fruity, caramelized, burnt-sugar flavor like the one you create by heating and caramelizing sugar.

These molecules are particularly cool because not only do they have a meaning and a function for the strawberry, but they have a meaning and function for us as well. For the plant, they're pure biochemistry, protecting the fruit from mold or attracting an animal that will be able to spread the seeds embedded in the fruit. For humans, though, these molecules serve a different purpose. They trigger sensations that our

"Flavor isn't just for certified sommeliers or coffee geeks—it's what we are made for and it connects all of us."

brains are hardwired to process in tandem with our emotions and memories. Most flavors we discern actually come from smell, and smell is very closely associated with memory storage and emotional recall; in fact, unlike most of the other senses, we process smell (and the smell-based part of flavor) through an emotional lens before we perceive it consciously. We're primed, when we eat the strawberry, to remember not only the flavors in the fruit, but how we felt and what we were doing when we experienced those flavors in the past. This makes flavor both intensely personal and a potent medium for connecting humans and transmitting culture. If we access memories and emotions every time we taste a familiar flavor, experiencing that flavor becomes a way to reinforce the emotional components of interpersonal bonds and identity building. The complexity of flavor—all of its sensations and emotional coloring—happens whether we're eating a strawberry, slurping Grandma's stew, or tasting a fine whiskey.

With a little chemistry knowledge, you can do this kind of deep analysis of flavor and molecules for almost anything—flavors that come from plants, like fruits or spices, but also flavors that come from transforming foods, like by searing, braising, or fermentation. Good cooks come to understand the contours and transformations of flavor simply by paying attention and trusting their experiential intuition. I've found real magic in translating the technical knowledge of flavor science for chefs and other food-makers and seeing where they run with it as they connect it to what they already know from taste-testing in the kitchen.

But flavor is something we all unconsciously experience and think about all the time. It's an emotional and individually unique phenomenon, which can feel ineffable and at times magical. Flavor is a compass for intuitive, associative, and expressive creativity. It's also a connector—to our memories and shared experiences in a brain-based way, and to evolution, ecologies, and landscapes in a tasteable way. Learning a bit about how flavor functions and how it connects to food and cooking can help you create more freely in the kitchen. And a strawberry is a great place to start.

Tanya Holland

TANYA HOLLAND IS the chef and owner of Brown Sugar Kitchen, a San Francisco Bay Area soul food institution since its doors first opened in Oakland in 2008. Renowned for her modern, West Coast–inspired interpretation of soul food, Holland creates dishes that plumb the complex history of African American food, such as her braised oxtail with North African spices, grits, and spinach.

Holland's culinary path began in New York City, where she worked in restaurants after graduating from college and was inspired to travel to France to pursue classical cooking training. After receiving her Grande Diplôme from La Varenne École de Cuisine in 1992, she returned to the United States to work in professional kitchens in Brooklyn, Boston, and Martha's Vineyard.

She competed on season fifteen of *Top Chef* in 2017 and has since made numerous appearances on *The Talk, Melting Pot*, and many other television shows. A prolific writer and speaker, Holland is the author of two cookbooks and talks openly about the many roadblocks she's faced throughout her career as an African American woman chef and her focus on building a more inclusive and equitable hospitality industry.

> "Everyone fails. It's the ones who persevere who ultimately win."

Holland at Brown
Sugar Kitchen in
Oakland, California

Sara Forte

Sara Forte is the writer behind the award-winning blog
Sprouted Kitchen *and a cookbook author based in*
Southern California. She is known for her healthful and
seasonal recipes, her passion for easygoing gatherings,
and her witty reflections on cooking and family life.

Grilled Wild Salmon Tacos

Serves 4

My kids will eat most things in taco or burrito format. During wild salmon season (usually May to September), tacos are our favorite way to eat the fish, and if friends are joining us, this recipe accommodates them beautifully. We roast a big slab of salmon and set out the tortillas, sauce, and fixings. A pot of beans on the side. It's a meal that everyone enjoys.

SALMON

Neutral oil, such as avocado, for oiling the grill grate, if grilling

2 tablespoons extra virgin olive oil or avocado oil

1 teaspoon chili powder

Dash of cayenne

1 tablespoon maple syrup

½ teaspoon ground cumin

¾ teaspoon sea salt

1½-pound fillet of wild salmon or fish of your choice

Juice of one large lime, to finish

AVOCADO SAUCE

2 cloves garlic, peeled

½ bunch cilantro, roughly chopped

1 jalapeño, mostly seeded, roughly chopped

¼ cup roasted pepitas

Juice of one large lime

3 tablespoons extra virgin olive oil

½ teaspoon sea salt, plus extra to taste

2 medium avocados, pitted

FOR SERVING

3 to 4 cups finely shredded cabbage

½ bunch cilantro, roughly chopped

Corn tortillas

6 scallions, roughly chopped

Toasted pepitas, for garnish

Hot sauce (optional)

Pickled onions (optional)

❶ Make the salmon: Clean and oil the grates. Heat your grill to medium-low. If the grill sounds like a hassle, preheat the oven to 375°F.

❷ In a small bowl, make a paste by mixing the 2 tablespoons olive oil, chili powder, cayenne, maple syrup, cumin, and salt. Rub it onto the flesh of the fish and let it sit for about 15 minutes.

❸ While you wait, make the avocado sauce: In a food processor or blender, combine the garlic, ½ bunch cilantro, jalapeño, ¼ cup pepitas, lime juice, 3 tablespoons olive oil, and salt, plus ½ cup water, and pulse a few times. Add the flesh of the avocados and pulse again until combined, but not completely pureed. (You're going for a consistency that's thinner than guacamole but thicker than salad dressing.) If it looks too thick, add lime juice or water to thin. Taste for seasoning and set aside. Store covered in the fridge if making the sauce in advance.

④ Grill the fillet (with the lid closed) to medium doneness, about 8 minutes. I don't like flipping the fish on the grill—it's a mess—so I just cook on one side until it's done. If you're using the oven, roast the salmon for 10 to 15 minutes (you can assume about 10 minutes per inch of thickness). Transfer the fish to a platter and let it rest for a few minutes. Squeeze the lime juice over the top of the fish and gently flake it apart to create the taco filling.

⑤ In a small bowl, toss the cabbage and ½ bunch cilantro with a bit of avocado sauce to coat. Warm the tortillas in a pan or over a flame. Assemble your tacos: Add a spoonful of sauce, a portion of fish, and generous topping of cabbage on top. Garnish with scallions, toasted pepitas, hot sauce, and pickled onions, if you've got them.

Note: The avocado sauce will keep in the fridge for 3 to 5 days.

"My kitchen is my headquarters, my office and refuge and playroom. A place to turn up the music and welcome people in or stir cookie dough with my babies or quietly cook alone and think. No place holds all the pieces of me quite like this one."

Christine Ha

CHRISTINE HA LIKES to say that she's a result of the courage and perseverance of her parents, who fled war-torn Vietnam in 1975, leaving everything they knew behind for the dream of a better life in America. Thinking back on her childhood in Southern California and Texas, Ha remembers that there was always an abundance of her mother's homemade food on the table.

When Ha was fourteen, her mother passed away. "I think humans are much stronger and more capable than we give ourselves credit for," she says. "When we survive one challenge, it prepares us for the next, builds character, and makes us more compassionate."

During college, Ha taught herself to cook, voraciously studying Vietnamese and Asian cookbooks to recreate the food her mother used to make for her without any recipes to follow. Cooking became a salve for her grief, a way to feel closer to her mother. When she discovered that her food could also bring others joy, she was hooked.

But it was at this time that Ha began to rapidly lose vision in her left eye. She was also experiencing temporary paralysis from the neck down, which led to a misdiagnosis of multiple sclerosis. Eventually her doctors discovered that she had neuromyelitis optica, a central nervous system disorder that affects the eye nerves and spinal cord. Though she regained function of her spine, she eventually lost all eyesight.

Determined to retain independence in her daily life, Ha quit her job as a software consultant, pursued a master's degree in creative writing (another life passion), and taught herself braille. A crucial part of regaining self-sufficiency was finding her way back to cooking for and feeding

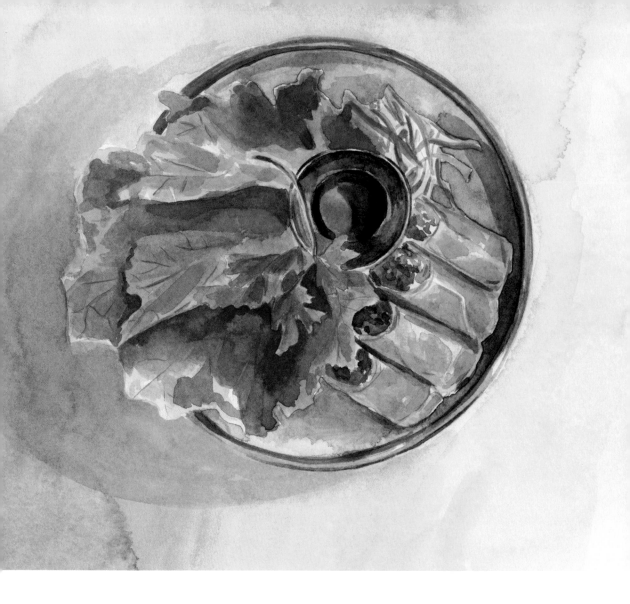

ABOVE

Ha's iteration of her mother's Vietnamese egg rolls

herself. After much trial and error in the kitchen, she gradually developed a heightened perception of taste, smell, touch, and sound. During her last semester of graduate school, her husband encouraged her to audition for season three of *MasterChef*. Though she was

hesitant, Ha thought the experience might yield great writing material, if nothing else, and decided to give it a try. In 2012, she became the show's first blind contestant, showcasing the Vietnamese food of her childhood and impressing judges and fans with her knife skills,

> "You can not speak the same language, not grow up in the same country, not share the same political views, but you can sit down at the same table and break bread together."

calm confidence, and deft reliance on her four senses. She went on to win the competition, defeating her seventeen fellow contestants, who had been chosen from a pool of thirty thousand home cooks.

Before competing on the show, Ha had grappled with self-confidence and often felt compelled to hide her blindness. After sharing her story on national television, she felt surprisingly free; by embracing her vulnerability, she had found a new strength and openness that allowed her to foster truly authentic connections with others—a source of continual inspiration in her life and work. Ha now speaks all over the world about her experience, and she shares various aspects of her life as a blind chef on social media and her YouTube cooking show and through her writing.

In 2019, she opened a restaurant in Houston called the Blind Goat, a modern Vietnamese gastropub.

Front and center on the menu is the first recipe Ha recreated from memory: her mother's Vietnamese egg rolls, made with pork, shrimp, garlic, shallot, onion, carrot, wood ear mushroom, mung bean noodles, and fish sauce. A tribute to her mother and to Ha's personal journey, they are one of the restaurant's most popular dishes. "I am thankful for all the challenges I went through because they made me into who I am today—a better person who is more determined and confident," says Ha. "I know I can survive pretty much anything that life throws at me."

IN CONVERSATION

Who is your mentor or hero?

"Definitely Mama Karen Washington, who started Black Urban Growers. When I was a young person, she encouraged me not to quit farming. When I was wondering if I was being a race traitor because there were so many white folks at the [farming] conferences and my people were working on housing issues and education issues, she was like, 'No, we have a place on the land and we need food for our people.'

"Also the Queen Mothers in Ghana, West Africa, who are the elders who really challenged me. They were like, 'In the US, is it true that a farmer puts a seed in the ground and doesn't pray, doesn't sing, doesn't pour libation, doesn't even say thank you, and expects the seed to grow?' They encouraged me to put the spiritual back into agriculture."

—Leah Penniman
cofounder, co-executive director, and farm manager
of Soul Fire Farm, educator, and food justice activist
Grafton, NY

"I am lucky to have several people I consider mentors, but a fairly consistent one is Jonathan Benno. I worked for Chef Benno at Per Se, fresh out of culinary school. He guided me through that experience and my subsequent career with sound advice and a sense of humor. I still reach out to him when I need a stern push in the right direction. My other heroes are Judy Rodgers, Alice Waters, and Renee Erickson. I admire those women for how incredibly hard they've worked to build foundational restaurants while making it look elegant and effortless."

—Julia Sullivan
chef, cofounder, and owner of Henrietta Red
Nashville, TN

"Magical Elves, the production company for *Top Chef*, was cofounded and run by an incredible woman, Jane Lipsitz. She is no longer with the company, but she has definitely been a mentor to me. Just watching her navigate the landscape and be such an impactful leader in her field has been inspiring to witness. She's successful and smart and strong and unapologetic about it, in the best ways. She also raised a wonderful family and stayed true to making the projects she's passionate about. She owns it and that's been so helpful for me to see."

—Gail Simmons
culinary expert, television personality, cofounder of
Bumble Pie Productions, and food writer
New York, NY

"My heroes are the unsung and invisible Black women who have made an indelible impact on American food culture. I hold a special place in my heart for the preserving and pickling power of Abby Fisher; the organizing power of farmer Fannie Lou Hamer; and the sensuous, rooted writing and recipes of Edna Lewis."

—Shakirah Simley
director of the Office of Racial Equity
for the City and County of San Francisco
and founder of Nourish | Resist
San Francisco, CA

"This is such a hard question for me. Honestly, I have had a number of people who may have taken me under their wing or helped me in some way, BUT I don't really have any specific person because there's just not a lot of humans like me. I have had to carve my own path. There was one Indian woman chef named Raji Jallepalli who I never got to meet because she died at the early age of fifty-two. She had a restaurant in Memphis in the '90s called Restaurant Raji, where she cooked French Indian food, and got two stars from William Grimes at the *New York Times* for being the chef of Tamarind restaurant in New York. I was gifted her cookbook, and it meant a lot to me because at the time there were so few (read: none) representations of Indian women cooking fine-dining food."

—Preeti Mistry
chef, entrepreneur, speaker, and activist
Oakland, CA

"When I went to culinary school, my instructor was an incredible woman named Catherine Pantsios. She's been in the business for over forty years and was a trailblazer in the early days of the Bay Area's 'California Cuisine' movement. Catherine was such an outstanding instructor that when I opened San Francisco Cooking School, she was the first person I hired. In her mid-sixties she was still running circles around young cooks in the kitchen. She is insatiably curious, hardworking, committed, kind, and diligent. Over twenty years later, I continue to hear her words and advice in my head all the time."

—Jodi Liano
founder and director of San Francisco Cooking
School, cooking instructor, and author
San Francisco, CA

"Any woman who has the courage to speak her truth, take big risks, and march to the beat of her own drum. Women who empower other women. Christine Blasey Ford, Ruth Bader Ginsburg, Gloria Steinem, Michelle Obama."

—Allie Balin
restaurant consultant, sommelier, and
cofounder of Henrietta Red
Lake Tahoe, CA

Alana Newhouse

Alana Newhouse is an author and the founder and editor in chief of Tablet *magazine, which explores Jewish news, ideas, and culture.*

My siblings and I were standing around my mother's bed. I was expected to utter the words. I was expected to say that her husband—the man with whom, for better or worse, her entire life had been intertwined for fifty-five years—had died.

That morning, I avoided crying by planning. *How late can the funeral be? Is there shiva on Friday night? Can my frail mother handle hordes of people stomping through her small apartment?* It had been seven years since she lived in the house they loved, among the community that was their extended family. His death marked the loss of the one thing about her domestic life that was still familiar to her. Of all the things Jewish tradition prepares one for, mourning in a vacuum is not one.

Bourekas.

I had to find her bourekas. The bourekas of her own Sephardic community; the bourekas that marked every Sabbath, every holiday, every rite of passage for us. They were the only thing I could think of that I knew she would both remember *and* be soothed by.

My mother is not from a huge Middle Eastern Sephardic community, the one with all the stores and the synagogues and the schools and the mansions in Brooklyn. Her people are Balkan Jews, Ladino-speaking Sephardim descended from those who fled Spain after the Inquisition—a minority inside a minority inside a minority. Turns out their bourekas are, too.

Her bourekas, our bourekas, are neither the dense half-moons nor the triangles of sesame-seeded dough. Instead, they are spirals—thick snakes of spinach and cheese gloved in the thinnest layer of phyllo dough. And they are actually called bollos, which I learned while calling kosher takeout places. Within an hour, staffers at three stores were texting me pictures of pastries still in their ovens, peek-a-boo shots taken almost surreptitiously. But none were right. The sun was setting on the day. The funeral was in eighteen hours.

Then, suddenly, there was a visual match. I ordered fifty.

After the funeral, I forced myself to have a taste. I was crestfallen. It was all wrong. The dough was thick and cottony, there was almost no filling, it needed *salt*—no Jewish dish ever needs *more* salt! It was like eating a tennis ball.

I suppose that's my way of explaining how I came to roll not one, not two, not three, but four batches of bollos for shiva, to give my mother something familiar at a deeply unfamiliar time. That night, at least a dozen spirals broke as I twisted them, and another half dozen burned because someone sent me a picture of my father in medical school and it stunned me so much that I finally fell apart. I made the last batch—the fourth one, which came closest to home—while weeping.

They were properly salted.

What do you cook when you're exhausted or short on time?

"'Refrigerator pasta,' aka pasta with whatever veggies are in the fridge plus pesto or tomato sauce made with garden ingredients. I keep batches in the freezer so it's ready to grab and defrost for quick meals."

—Whitney
Bozeman, MT

"I think I'm not allowed to say I order in? Or that I *always* feel short on time and exhausted? One go-to is shrimp pasta with grape tomatoes and wilted spinach, plus lots of salt, pasta water, olive oil, and Parmesan. We also eat lots of carnitas in tacos with guacamole, cheese, and sour cream and corn on the cob or black beans."

—Chantal
Oakland, CA

"My grandmother's 'Garbage Soup.' Start with sautéed onion, celery, carrots, and garlic, and add anything in the refrigerator (leftovers are great) or pantry that fits your mood. Add chicken broth and simmer. Always delicious."

—Janice
Indianapolis, IN

"Pasta, pasta, pasta."

—Susie
Auburn, CA

"Chicken or shrimp fajitas with plenty of assorted veggies."

—Marion
Bishopville, MD

"It's always pasta with a lot of umami, Parmesan cheese or anchovies, and bread crumbs and some easy-to-steam veggies on the side, drizzled with olive oil and lemon."

—Linnea
Los Angeles, CA

"Emergency spaghetti: I throw a pound of pasta, a jar of pasta sauce, water, and frozen meatballs in the Instant Pot and walk away."

—Leah
Seattle, WA

What do you cook when you're energized or have plenty of time?

"Any sort of Asian-inspired dish or something from one of the Ottolenghi cookbooks."

—Whitney
Bozeman, MT

"When I'm energized and have lots of time, I'd choose to do something other than cook! I always treat cooking as something that needs to be quick and pretty healthy and can create an experience for our family to be together and connect. The cooking itself generally doesn't provide relaxation—it's the chance to sit and eat together that does."

—Chantal
Oakland, CA

"Middle Eastern stews often including eggplant, chickpeas, cumin, fresh ginger, turmeric, garlic, and a pinch of cayenne, or as much as my husband will tolerate."

—Janice
Indianapolis, IN

"Long, complicated Parisian recipes."

—Susie
Auburn, CA

"I like to cook traditional family recipes that bring me warm memories of my mother and grandmother. These include prime rib with Yorkshire pudding, crab imperial, Granny's stewed tomatoes, coq au vin and French bread, frozen strawberry soufflé with Grand Marnier sauce, strawberry shortcake, and hot fudge sundaes."

—Marion
Bishopville, MD

"Something I've never made before, and if it's during the fall or winter, that's usually some type of soup."

—Linnea
Los Angeles, CA

"I roast a lovely chicken and make several seasonal vegetables on the side."

—Leah
Seattle, WA

Annie Happel

Annie Happel is a self-described seeker of all things delicious based in San Francisco. She has worn many hats in the food world, including those of writer, publicist, marketer, and blogger.

The Blue Dress Cookbook

My sister and I took turns designing the covers and title pages for The Blue Dress Cookbook, our family's (somewhat) annual holiday gift for family and friends. My mom was the editor in chief, author, publisher, and distributor, while the rest of us benefited from her recipe testing throughout the years.

I loved drawing the cookbook covers until around age eleven, when I internalized a shameful fifth-grade art class experience that involved drawing a bird freehand. After that, I decided that I wasn't good at drawing, so the cookbook cover was no longer appealing. Instead of fretting about the composition of a snowflake, I channeled my energy into food.

It would take me more than a decade to connect the dots and recognize that I love cooking, in large part because I was raised by an exceptional cook and cookbook sorceress. In my twenties, I spent time farming in Spain and France to better understand how food grows and started my own blog, *Happelsauce*, to record my experiences on the farms. It quickly turned into the online, next-generation version of The Blue Dress Cookbook, filled with my favorite recipes and stories. Instead of grade-school cover art, *Happelsauce* was graced with amateur food photos, poorly lit and completely unstyled. But I loved it. My mom has always been my biggest fan, commenting on almost every post, cooking from my recipes, and sharing the links with her friends. Just the other day, an old friend told me that my Wintertime Wonderful Lentil Soup was served for hundreds of guests at her friend's

wedding last year, per his request. That made my day.

The last Blue Dress was compiled by my mom in 2014, and *Happelsauce* has been defunct since 2016, when our daughter Lucie turned six months old. She is now closing in on three and a half, and I'm pregnant with our second child. I still cook quite a bit, but I no longer carve out the time to snap food photos and write. These days, once the dishes are done, I'm in bed. Gone are the nights of writing into the wee hours. My life feels full in ways I couldn't have imagined, and time is elusive. I work in restaurant publicity, and my partner is a chef and restaurateur. We live above one

of his restaurants. Probably none of this is a coincidence. After all, for me, food is love.

I have thought, wistfully, about writing a cookbook that pays homage to The Blue Dress and my mom. It would be a collaborative effort, really. I would start by cooking old favorites from The Blue Dress Cookbooks, then share notes and stories with my mom, our conversations spanning one time zone and more than a thousand miles from California to Montana, recalling our favorite meals from the last few decades. It feels big and daunting on one hand, and so obvious on the other.

Food connects and unites us. It can be both deeply optimistic and reassuring. I believe there is power and healing in inviting everyone into the kitchen, and a good cookbook can inspire just that.

Nite Yun

NITE YUN WAS born in a refugee camp in Thailand, where her parents met after escaping Cambodia's Khmer Rouge genocide in the 1970s. In 1984, the family came to the United States and settled in Stockton, California, where there was a large Cambodian community. Yun often helped her mother prepare traditional Cambodian food, her first introduction to the country's flavors.

After high school, Yun moved to San Francisco to study nursing. Though the city offered a wealth of restaurants, it was hard to find one that replicated the Cambodian food she had grown up eating, so she taught herself to cook by using her mom's recipes. Eventually, Yun left nursing school and embarked on a series of trips to Cambodia, returning periodically to San Francisco to work odd jobs. With each visit, she discovered more about her heritage and the country's vibrant prewar culture and intricate Khmer cuisine. Inspired by everything she learned, Yun joined San Francisco's La Cocina incubator program in 2014 and worked to develop her cooking skills and create a business plan for her future restaurant.

Four years later, Yun opened Nyum Bai (Khmer for "let's eat," a phrase often used by her mother) in Oakland, California. The restaurant's street food–inspired fare honors 1960s and '70s Cambodia, a period when rock music, classical dance, and Boran cinema (films based on traditional Cambodian legends) thrived in Phnom Penh, before the Khmer Rouge regime's violent censorship of intellectuals and artists. At Nyum Bai, Cambodian rock is on constant rotation, vintage record album covers adorn the walls, and Yun's flavorful food is plated up with care—all in tribute to the country's "golden era" and a reminder of the beauty and strength that preceded tragedy.

Kroeung

Makes a bowlful

Kroeung is the first Khmer recipe I learned from my mom. Kroeung is everything; it's great with any sauté, or perfect as a marinade. For an easy dinner, add some fish sauce or oyster sauce for additional flavor and throw it in with any stir-fried veggies and protein or add it to soup. Very simple but delicious!

Using a large mortar and pestle, smash the lemongrass until it has a fine and paste-like texture. Add the rest of the ingredients and continue smashing until a paste forms.

3 pounds lemongrass, outer layers removed, inner layers minced

8 ounces galangal root, peeled and chopped

1½ ounces makrut lime leaves

1 pound garlic cloves, peeled and roughly chopped

8 ounces minced shallots

4 bird's eye chili peppers, destemmed and thoroughly washed

Thumb-size piece of fresh turmeric root, roughly chopped and bruises cut off

What fuels your passion for vegetables?

"My love of vegetables is rooted in my history as a gardener. I grow my own food and find the vegetable garden to be a place of constant personal evolution. Like cooking, growing edible plants is not about mastery. I am always a student, expanding my palate and technique every single time I step into the garden. There are not many things I can be sure I will never tire of in my life, but healthy eating is definitely one."

—Julia Sherman
creator of Salad for President and writer
Los Angeles, CA

"I'm committed to creating more progressive farm policies, including workers' rights, as well as mitigating food waste, which both honors the work it takes to grow food and affects climate change."

—Abra Berens
chef at Granor Farm and author
Three Oaks, MI

"We all deserve to be treated with compassion and loving-kindness. We can direct this love to ourselves by choosing to eat foods that nourish our cells. We can direct the love to the planet by learning about the impact our food choices have on the environment. Or, for some of us, there's a calling to share this loving-kindness with animals by following a plant-based way of eating. I love making meals centered around this because I love the message of compassion that comes with it."

—Sadia Badiei
BSc Dietetics and founder of Pick Up Limes
Eindhoven, Netherlands

"Community organizing and showing people what veganism can look like for folks of color and why we should care about animals, our health, and how environmental racism affects us all in different ways. I started Veggie Mijas, a women of color and nonbinary folks of color collective, to start having conversations about our marginalized identities and our plant-based lifestyles. I believe educating folks of color on how to grow their own food, get involved in their community gardens, and cook simple, plant-based recipes truly goes a long way."

—Amy Quichiz
founder of Veggie Mijas, writer, and activist
New York, NY

What season do you anticipate with the most excitement?

"Late summer, for sure! I think people on the East Coast get prematurely excited about produce in the spring and early summer. In reality, summer produce doesn't really start popping off until the end of summer, when it's last call for tomatoes and the farmers can hardly give them away."

—Julia Sherman
creator of Salad for President and writer
Los Angeles, CA

"I love autumn. Summer is wonderful and frenetic and stuffed to the gills. In fall, food is at its best and most diverse, and the weather is cool enough to want to cook, and everyone's schedules are a bit more orderly, making it easier to find the time to cook together."

—Abra Berens
chef at Granor Farm and author
Three Oaks, MI

"I'm a sun-chaser. Summer fruits like berries and melons are my absolute favorite. Iced drinks, smoothies, and BBQs in the park—they all give me those cozy summertime feelings and remind me of the beach, holidays, and time spent exploring the great outdoors. Winter is a close second. In the Netherlands, there is the word 'gezellig,' which encompasses the heart of the Dutch culture. It includes everything that is cozy, warm, and inviting. There is nothing more gezellig than the feeling of being inside with family and friends, having a good laugh, and enjoying a comforting meal. While I might not love the cold outside, I do love the coziness that comes with it."

—Sadia Badiei
BSc Dietetics and founder of Pick Up Limes
Eindhoven, Netherlands

"Fall, because that is the richest time for produce. It's something of a shoulder season when you get, say, the first of the winter squash and the last of the eggplant. I find that a very exciting time to cook and eat. After that, local food choices narrow—at least they do in New Mexico. But fall is a very luxurious time everywhere."

—Deborah Madison
chef, cooking teacher, master gardener, and author
Galisteo, NM

Deborah Madison

CHEF DEBORAH MADISON was decades ahead of her time when she opened her influential restaurant Greens in San Francisco in 1979. One of the first farm-driven restaurants in the Bay Area, Greens is often credited with transforming vegetarian food into sophisticated cuisine.

Raised on a dairy farm in upstate New York and a walnut orchard in Davis, California, Madison developed a keen interest in and familiarity with plants, farms, and farmers. She is widely recognized for her work with seasonal vegetables, especially heritage varieties and heirloom grains, but prefers not to be limited by the vegetarian label. The heart of her passion is connecting people to the sources and stories of their food, and she has pursued that in a variety of ways: through writing (she is the author of fourteen cookbooks and a memoir); as a student and chef at San Francisco Zen Center; in founding Greens and, later, Café Escalera in Santa Fe; through her work with the Slow Food movement and Seed Savers Exchange (an organization that collects and preserves heirloom seeds and plants); and as a master gardener and cooking teacher. For more than twenty years, Madison has lived in Galisteo, New Mexico, where she continues to work with local farmers markets, write, garden, and teach.

LEFT

Madison cooking greens in her kitchen

> "I love vegetables because they have histories and stories, because they are beautiful and sometimes odd, because they taste good and are interesting to work with."

Niki Nakayama

1. SAKI ZUKE:
Amaebi, caviar, smoked avocado, sanbaizu gelée

BORN TO JAPANESE
immigrants in Los Angeles, Niki Nakayama felt called to explore her parents' home country very early in her career. After graduating from culinary school, she embarked on a three-year tour of Japan to learn about the country's cuisine while working in restaurants. It was on this journey that she first experienced and fell in love with kaiseki, a traditional and elaborate Japanese meal that emphasizes balance, seasonality, texture, and appearance through the presentation of many small, artful courses.

Nakayama describes her introduction to kaiseki as an "unfolding of gifts with each plate, little by little." The experience was transformative, and she decided to learn all she could about the art form to share its joys with others.

2. ZENSAI:
Ebi shinjo, hotaru ika, enoki tempura, uni junsai, mozuku, miyazaki Wagyu cannoli, strawberry

But because the practice is steeped in centuries-old tradition and gender segregation is still prevalent in much of Japanese culture, "99 percent of people who get to do it professionally are men," Nakayama explains. "In Japan, the culinary world is a field that is known for its craft, technique, and tradition, and women are often thought of as incapable of working at these high standards."

ABOVE, RIGHT, AND PAGES 164–165

Twelve courses from n/naka's late June 2019 menu

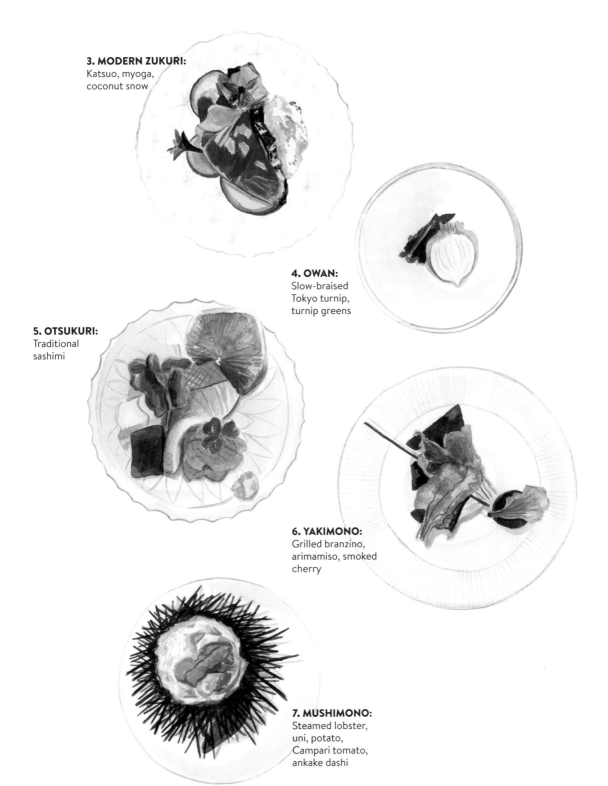

3. MODERN ZUKURI:
Katsuo, myoga,
coconut snow

4. OWAN:
Slow-braised
Tokyo turnip,
turnip greens

5. OTSUKURI:
Traditional
sashimi

6. YAKIMONO:
Grilled branzino,
arimamiso, smoked
cherry

7. MUSHIMONO:
Steamed lobster,
uni, potato,
Campari tomato,
ankake dashi

8. SHIIZAKANA:
Spaghetti, abalone,
pickled cod roe,
truffles

9. NIKU:
A5 miyazaki
Wagyu beef,
snap pea, pea
tendrils

Undeterred, she trained in Japan at Shirakawa-Ya Ryokan, her cousin's inn, under chef Masa Sato and then returned to California. In 2011, she opened her kaiseki restaurant, n/naka, which has since become one of Los Angeles's most critically acclaimed restaurants. "California kaiseki," as Nakayama lovingly calls it, is a blend of her American upbringing and her Japanese heritage and training.

Nakayama operates n/naka with her wife and sous chef, Carole Iida-Nakayama, and a staff of mostly women. "I've always believed that a restaurant like ours, being owned by women, doing the kind of food that we do, would have a hard time finding the right audience in a place like Japan," she reflects. "I feel very accepted here." And that's why n/naka's location is ideal: "Kaiseki really is about wanting to show appreciation for the landscape and the nature that surrounds you. It's so much about gratitude. What better place to do it than in California, where the seafood is amazing, the produce is amazing, the seasonality is not like it is in other places," says Nakayama.

10. SUNOMONO:
Cucumber, wakame,
grapes

11. SHOKUJI:
Nigiri sushi

"After you've been doing something for a good amount of time, it becomes a part of who you are and you're able to use that knowledge you've built over time to allow the expression to come through a little bit more clearly. With the creative process, I've always felt that the more I trust it, the more it feels right."

12. MIZUMONO:
Tomato sorbet,
green tomato kanten,
cucumber and lime
granita, kuro goma
pudding, shiro goma
cream, almond brisée,
strawberries, puffed
rice

IN CONVERSATION

What kitchen tools do you love most?

"Silicone spatulas. I hate waste, and a good spatula ensures that not one spoonful will be wasted!"

—Mimi Mendoza
pastry chef at Senia
Honolulu, HI

"I don't know where I would be without the many devices I have to squeeze citrus. My mother had me squeeze so many lemons as a kid (for her Middle Eastern catering company) that I'm truly traumatized by it, so now I appreciate any and all assistance I can get. I use lots of citrus in Middle Eastern cooking, so this is really important to me!"

—Rose Previte
restaurateur and owner of
Maydān and Compass Rose
Washington, DC

"Probably Le Creuset pots—you can use them for preserving; you can use them for braising. They're extraordinary. I have had some of them for thirty years."

—Joyce Goldstein
chef, restaurant consultant, and author
San Francisco, CA

"I have three things that I love equally: 1) A Microplane, because it's so versatile. You can use it to grate cheese, nutmeg, and chocolate, or even garlic or ginger, and to zest citrus. 2) A sharpening stone. Nothing is worse than working with a dull knife. 3) Parchment paper."

—Barbara Lynch
chef and owner of Barbara Lynch Collective
Boston, MA

"One time my mom asked me if it was strange that the only thing she loved more than her KitchenAid mixer was my dad, and I inherited that love (of both my dad and my mixer). Baking is how I relax and my very favorite pastime, so I know that any time spent hanging with my KitchenAid is time spent doing what I love."

—Jodi Liano
founder and director of San Francisco Cooking School,
cooking instructor, and author
San Francisco, CA

RECIPE BY

Ashley Rodriguez

As the cocreator, coproducer, and host of the James Beard Award–nominated series Kitchen Unnecessary, *Ashley Rodriguez takes viewers through the wild reaches of the American Northwest, where she forages and hunts for unusual and place-specific ingredients with local guides, experts, and friends. Each installment culminates with Rodriguez gathering her guests around the campfire or picnic table to create a beautiful meal that celebrates the prized ingredients they found together.*

Morel Toast
with Charred Ramp Aioli

Serves 4

Morels, readily available in the spring, are heralded as one of the most delicious mushrooms. For me it's not just because of their taste—woody, meaty, and almost truffle-like—but also because of how these fire or burn morels, as they are commonly called, grow every spring after forest fires raged through the woods the previous summer. It's the perfect illustration of the earth caring for itself and for us.

❶ Once the morels have been acquired, it's time to start the fire. (It seems fitting to prepare these morels over fire.) Drizzle the bread slices with 2 tablespoons of the olive oil. Set a grill grate over hot coals, then grill the bread until the edges are charred and the exterior is crisp while the interior stays nice and soft. Set the bread aside.

❷ Set the ramps on the grill grate and cook until wilted and charred in parts, 2 to 3 minutes, then flip and repeat. Set those aside to cool, then roughly chop and stir into the mayonnaise to make the ramp aioli. Add a hefty pinch of sea salt and set aside.

❸ Set a large cast-iron skillet directly on the hot coals and add the remaining tablespoon of olive oil. Add the morels and a hefty pinch of sea salt, then sauté, stirring frequently, until the morels are deeply caramelized.

❹ Slather a good bit of the ramp aioli onto the crisp pieces of toast, then add the warm morels on top. Finish with a flurry of chopped herbs and edible flowers, then marvel at the bounty that is gifted to us from the earth. Enjoy immediately.

4 thick slices country bread

3 tablespoons olive oil

1 bunch ramps or scallions

1 cup mayonnaise

Sea salt

8 ounces morels, roughly chopped

Freshly chopped herbs, such as chives and/or parsley

Edible flowers (herb flowers, calendula, borage, marigold, lavender, nasturtium, dandelion, pansy)

"Whenever you get a bunch of people at a table, you learn about the people at that table. The young folks learn about their elders, they learn about their culture, and listen to stories about the past. I feel this responsibility to educate people through my cooking."

—Mashama Bailey
partner and executive chef at The Grey

ESSAY BY

Elaine Chukan Brown

Elaine Chukan Brown is a wine writer whose work has been featured in Food & Wine *and* Wine & Spirits *magazines, among other publications, and on JancisRobinson.com. In 2019, she was named one of the "Most Inspiring People in Wine" by the Wine Industry Network. She is also known for her illustrated tasting notes, which she began creating in her early days of learning about wine and still enjoys making to this day.*

Fishing, Philosophy, and Wine

My family is from Alaska, all the way back. My mother's side is Unangan from the Bristol Bay region, my father's Inupiaq from Norton Sound. My great-grandparents were full Unangan (or Aleut, as the outsiders named them). They were the ones who first encountered non-Native outsiders in their part of Alaska and went from fishing for subsistence to fishing for cash. Their lives made our lives possible.

I was nine when I started commercial fishing for salmon. Four generations fished together. As a Native person, I was raised to respect my elders. It is a culture that recognizes the value of life experience and wisdom earned, of community building and service given. My role was to absorb the elders' insights and stories, but also to learn the practice of their craft. After my great-grandparents retired, I started my own commercial fishing business at the age of thirteen.

By twenty-three, my desire to explore the rest of the world took hold. I sold my fishing business and eventually become an academic philosopher, doing doctoral work before taking a full-time faculty job. Teaching at the university level felt parallel to learning from my elders: As a researcher and educator, I learned from the experts before

me and translated that knowledge to my students.

But eventually, academic life became difficult in the United States. The 2008 financial crisis led to deep budget cuts at universities, increasing the workload for faculty and making it harder to effectively work with students. Over several years, the changes wore on me.

Finally, I decided to take a risk, leave my academic career, and start writing and speaking about wine. I saw wine as an opportunity to engage my curiosity about the world and other cultures and, in the case of family-owned or historic wineries, to listen to and gather stories of experience like I had been so privileged to do with my

Chukan Brown
in conversation
with a California
winemaker

The *Elaine Christine*,
Chukan Brown's
family's fishing boat

great-grandparents. Wine, for me, served as a way to marry the intellectual practice of philosophy with the study of craftsmanship.

Initially, I approached my wine work as if I were in grad school again. But the time I spent in wineries and vineyards with the people growing and making the wine— the elders of the industry, if you will—was the source of my studies, rather than books. In the midst of learning about geography, plant biology, climatology, soil science, and chemistry (all relevant to the growing and making of wine), I was also absorbing regional histories and life stories of producers. There was the couple in Italy who rescued grape varieties lost during the world wars by finding feral vines while hiking the mountains outside their village. The man in Spain who spent years driving around the outskirts of deserted villages, looking for vineyards abandoned after the Spanish Civil War. The family in Oregon who were the first to plant vines in their region and establish varieties that would later become the hallmarks of the state's industry. As I lost my great-grandparents to age, vintners around the world formed a community in which I took on a new version of the cultural role I had held growing up.

As disparate as commercial fishing, philosophy, and wine are from each other, they offer me the opportunity to respect my elders by sharing the stories of others' life experiences and wisdom earned.

Gail Simmons

ORIGINALLY FROM TORONTO, Ontario, Gail Simmons grew up in a family "who saw the world through the lens of food." Her mother, a food writer for Canada's largest newspaper, loved to cook and entertain, and her family traveled extensively. After attending culinary school, Simmons trained in famed New York City kitchens Le Cirque 2000 and Vong, assisted *Vogue* food critic Jeffrey Steingarten, and joined *Food & Wine* magazine as a columnist and director of special events.

Simmons assembling a salad in her kitchen in Brooklyn, New York. "I spend a lot of time doing meal prep so I can set myself up to cook easily throughout the week," she says.

"Food is everywhere. It penetrates everything—our politics, sociology, anthropology. It's the way we nurture ourselves, our family, our friends. It's the way we entertain, the way we socialize. It's the way we connect with others, the way we explain our culture, celebrate our milestones. And there are always so many more delicious things to eat. . . . Food is a unifier."

In 2006, Simmons became a permanent judge on *Top Chef*, the Emmy award–winning reality TV food series that has aired for seventeen seasons and counting, with a worldwide audience. In 2014, Simmons and her business partner, Samantha Hanks, cofounded Bumble Pie Productions, a television production company dedicated to empowering women's voices in food and lifestyle entertainment, both in front of and behind the camera. "When I think about when I went to culinary school and first started cooking in restaurants as a line cook, it's amazing how much has changed. I was the only woman in both kitchens and I was not treated incredibly well. We've made great strides in this regard. And it is going to take many more years to get to a place of true equality, if we do at all. I hope that the earth is around for us to see it! But I think that every generation and every new class of women comes in stronger and better at asking for what they need, willing to compromise less and be louder about it. It's a hard glass ceiling that we are trying to break. It may be slow going, and it's hard to have patience when you're frustrated by it. But it's important work."

What legacy do you hope to create with your life's work?

"Certainly my books are part of my legacy, but that means not only the ones that I've written or contributed to, but also the [more than six thousand] books I've used for research. I'm also a pack rat and consider myself the custodian of the one hundred years' worth of African American history I've inherited: papers, photos, memorabilia, and more. The students I've taught in my fifty-year career as a college teacher are also part of my legacy, as are the food historians I've mentored or responded to over the years. It really is too much to think about, so I prefer instead to look ahead to the next projects; if I accomplish them, they'll add to my legacy, however it's defined."

—Jessica B. Harris
culinary historian, professor emerita,
journalist, speaker, and author
Brooklyn, NY; New Orleans, LA; and
Martha's Vineyard, MA

"Eventually I will grow old and be forgotten and my desserts will go out of fashion, but my cooks will be my legacy. A majority of pastry cooks are young women. The world and the restaurant industry have proven to be unkind. I just want to make sure they are strong and know how to fight for themselves in the industry and in life. And I hope they'll instill the same discipline and compassion I showed them in others, because honestly, what else matters?"

—Mimi Mendoza
pastry chef at Senia
Honolulu, HI

"I hope that South Asian people and South Asian food will get the representation they deserve in media. I hope that Indian food becomes part of mainstream American home cooking. I hope that future generations never have to hear people say 'chai tea' or 'naan bread' ever again."

—Priya Krishna
writer and author
New York, NY

"A deeper understanding of Japanese food for the rest of the world."

—Niki Nakayama
chef and owner of n/naka
Los Angeles, CA

"I want people to remember that we are the original people who were plant-based before the word 'veganism' was slapped on the front of packages; to remember that our ancestors had so much knowledge of our soil and earth; to remember our roots and why food justice should be so important to us. I want the legacy of our work to be shared, to bring people together in and outside of their kitchens."

—Amy Quichiz
founder of Veggie Mijas, writer, and activist
New York, NY

"We envision a more approachable and inclusive wine industry, and the purpose of our work is to unite and inspire people from all walks of life. That's not how we found the wine industry, but we hope to leave it that way for future generations."

—Robin McBride (president) **&
Andréa McBride John** (CEO)
cofounders of McBride Sisters Wine Collection
Oakland, CA

"I hope to inspire those who want to find a sense of purpose in their work. I also hope to be part of the rising tide that's transforming the food industry into a resilient community that lifts people up."

—Reem Assil
chef and owner of Reem's California,
entrepreneur, and activist
Oakland and San Francisco, CA

"I hope to show my daughter that she can be anything she sets her mind to, and I want to inspire the upcoming generation to work hard, ask questions, and dream big."

—Barbara Lynch
chef and owner of Barbara Lynch Collective
Boston, MA

Cara Mangini

Cara Mangini is a restaurateur, chef, and author based in Columbus, Ohio. After growing up in the San Francisco Bay Area surrounded by a food-loving family, Mangini worked at restaurants in New York and Napa Valley, where she became passionate about cooking with fresh, seasonal produce.

Charting the Seasons

Spring

Ramps—green, easy, packed with strong, fresh flavor—mark the first sign of spring in Ohio. They are a reward after a winter of breaking down local rutabaga and stubborn winter squashes, and a welcome sign of everything to come. Ramp pesto couscous with currants, almonds, and arugula is my spring favorite.

For me, artichokes capture the essence of spring in Northern California—they're grown on the coast near where I am from. My favorite artichoke recipe is my grandmother's artichoke torta (originally created by her mother). It's not traditional to the region of Italy on the Ligurian coast where my great-grandmother once lived, so

I'm sure it was inspired by the new life she created in California. My grandmother fed it to me, and now it feeds my children and brings me home.

Summer

Zucchini grows bountifully in my garden and in my mom's backyard. I use it to make zucchini, sweet corn, and tomato pasta garnished with basil and Parmesan. Ingredients in their prime make for simple, outrageously good food that is just as much about flavor and pleasure (and a connection to nature) as it is about supporting our health. This pasta is a perfect, light-filled, warm summer night.

When I think of the most perfect summer tomatoes, I think of heirloom tomatoes like the ones I harvested at Long Meadow Ranch in Napa Valley, an organic farm and wine producer that inspired so much of my work with vegetables. They are best when just-picked and sliced, with a sprinkle of Maldon sea salt and a drizzle of California olive oil.

Fall

Delicata squash is the first of the winter squash harvest, always arriving as a surprise before you are ready for summer to end. Roasted delicata squash and kale with quinoa, pepitas, and citrus vinaigrette tastes like that moment when the sun shifts angles and summer meets fall. It gets you in the mood for cooler days.

Whenever I eat sweet potatoes, I'm amazed that something pulled out of the dirt can taste so sweet. Sweet potato latkes with cranberry-chipotle compote are a new tradition I have brought to my family's holiday table and one I hope my children will someday request as a must-have at holiday meals.

Winter

I use organically grown rutabagas from Sunbeam Family Farms and store them through the Ohio winter. They are always one of the last vegetables standing. I featured them in rutabaga apple cakes with brussels sprouts and cabbage slaw, a dish I made while seven months pregnant at the James Beard House on International Women's Day in March 2018, a career highlight.

I love the beautifully imperfect, gnarly-looking organic celery root from Wayward Seed Farm. Celery root pot pie is a recipe I developed for my cookbook, *The Vegetable Butcher,* during an Ohio snowstorm—a California girl finding comfort and home in the Midwest. It's now and forever a recipe I make with and for my kids.

"I always knew that magic happened at the table surrounded by the people I love. That all started with my grandmothers, their mothers, and my mother."

SUMMER

SPRING

FALL

WINTER

Mutsuko Soma

GROWING UP IN Tochigi Prefecture, Japan, Mutsuko Soma watched her grandmother make notoriously tricky soba for family dinners with only one arm (she had lost the other arm in an accident). Years later, Soma moved to Seattle to attend culinary school. After graduating, she cooked at several restaurants in the city and became inspired to return to Japan to learn how to make the soba of her childhood. She went to Tokyo and enrolled in an intensive two-year course on the art of traditional soba making. During her studies, she discovered that Washington State was among the largest producers of buckwheat (a main ingredient in soba) in the United States—a fact that affirmed her desire to settle there.

When she returned to Seattle, Soma founded a pop-up restaurant called Kamonegi—a reference to the Japanese symbolization of a duck carrying a leek as the good fortune of one nice thing bringing another—to test soba's appeal. Her cooking quickly developed a cult following, and in 2017, Soma opened Kamonegi's brick-and-mortar restaurant to much acclaim. Now, Soma's young daughter watches as she expertly mixes, kneads, and cuts fresh, velvety soba every day, a nod to the genesis of Soma's own love affair with the craft.

Soma's Soba

Here, Soma shares her step-by-step process for making traditional soba.

1 I use a ratio of 20 percent all-purpose flour and 80 percent buckwheat flour, which I sift into the lacquered bowl. Water is added slowly, and I hold my fingers in a claw to mix it into the flours. The goal is to evenly moisturize each granule of flour so that the flour becomes coarse and crumbly, about the size of small pebbles.

2 I bring these pebbles together to form the dough. The repetitive motion of kneading the dough will eventually fold the sides of the soba dough inward to create a shape that resembles the chrysanthemum flower. We call this step kikuneri, and it helps squeeze out any air bubbles from the dough. I turn the chrysanthemum shape on its side and begin to roll with my hands until the flower takes on a conical shape. Once I start to roll this out, the point of the cone is where the center will be.

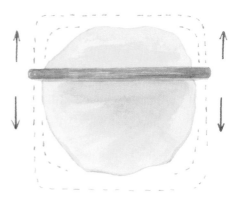

3 Using a rolling pin, I push down on the tip of the cone and begin rolling it into a flat circle. Once the dough has flattened sufficiently, I roll it onto the rolling pin and then roll the pin forward so that the edges of the dough roll over themselves and smack the table as they unroll. I do this in a rhythmic way, creating a *thwap thwap thwap* sound, repeating the motion ten to fifteen times and then turning the pin diagonally to develop a new edge. As the edges of the dough circle hit the table, I stretch them to create four corners. Eventually the dough unfurls from the pin to become a square.

❹ The surface area of this square is usually larger than the surface area of our table, so I unroll the dough halfway to work on one side. I use another rolling pin to further flatten this half. Then I turn the rolling pin around to unfurl and work on the other half. This additional rolling across the surface of the dough helps create a light, airy texture in the noodle. I roll the entire surface out very thin, to about a twentieth of an inch.

❺ Once all the dough is rolled out, I dust it with cornstarch to prevent sticking and fold the large square into thirds. With the cutting guide sitting on top of the folded dough, I begin cutting with the soba kiri (a single-bevel knife that cuts the noodle on one side while the other side follows the wooden guide). This motion makes a *kun-tink, kun-tink, kun-tink* sound. I make ten to fifteen cuts to produce about one portion of noodles. I store the completed portions in an airtight container in the refrigerator (fresh noodles are perishable and must be kept cool). They keep for about a day.

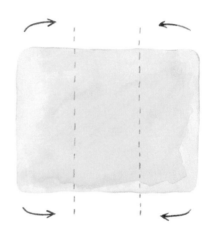

CUTTING GUIDE   SOBA KIRI

"My grandmother got in an accident and lost one of her arms, but she would harvest mushrooms from the mountains and grow her own food. Because of that, the importance of food became clear to me."

RIGHT

Kamo seiro—cold noodles served with hot duck soup, scallions, and wasabi—is Soma's favorite way to eat soba.

If you could eat a meal with one person, who would you choose and what would you eat together?

"Julia Child, and we would eat coq au vin. I was one of those nerdy kids who would watch her show on PBS. When I was in sixth grade I made my first Baked Alaska. I received her cookbooks as a birthday gift, and they were really life-changing for me. All I wanted to do was to get my ass to France so I could eat this food."

—**Martha Hoover**
restaurateur and founder of Patachou Inc.
and the Patachou Foundation
Indianapolis, IN

"I would sit down to eat with my mother, who passed away some years ago. We would have her red pozole for lunch."

—**Rosio Sanchez**
chef and owner of Hija de Sanchez
and Sanchez Cantina
Copenhagen, Denmark

"My partner, Mary Attea. She loves food as much as I do. We would have omakase, because we're obsessed with sushi."

—**Anita Lo**
chef, culinary tour guide, and author
New York, NY

"My father and my mother on Thanksgiving. Some years it was just the three of us; some years I would bring folks home from hither, thither, and yon. We had guests from Senegal, and guests from Benin, and relatives that came. But the three of us were certainly the nucleus."

—Jessica B. Harris
culinary historian, professor emerita,
journalist, speaker, and author
Brooklyn, NY; New Orleans, LA; and
Martha's Vineyard, MA

"Maya Angelou. In addition to writing masterful poetry, she authored two cookbooks. My admiration for her started when I was a teenager after I read *I Know Why the Caged Bird Sings*. I was enchanted by all the advice she dispensed over her long life. Both our grandmothers cooked directly from their gardens. I would love to sit down to dinner with her and tell her about my grandmother and hear about hers. I would cook some of my favorite recipes from my grandmother, and she could make a few of her grandmother's recipes. I'd listen to her speak about the importance of breaking bread and coming together."

—Anna Francese Gass
chef, recipe tester, and food writer
New York, NY

Bonnie Tsui

Journalist and author Bonnie Tsui approaches life with curiosity and zest, whether she's researching a story, cooking with her family, traveling, or surfing. Her writing explores the intersection of food, culture, and identity. In 2015, along with San Francisco's incubator kitchen La Cocina, she helped launch F&B: Voices from the Kitchen, *a biannual performance that shares the stories and perspectives of chefs and kitchens that are often overlooked.*

Ginger

The other night I was having dinner at a friend's house when she brought out the main dish: bo ssam, a sumptuous, fall-off-the-bone Korean pork dish, accompanied by a classic ginger-scallion sauce. At that moment the pork itself ceased to be the main event, at least for me. Rather, it was the simple, lucid flavor and aroma of the freshly chopped ginger mingling with the light soy sauce and the bite of the scallion that stepped forward to greet me like an old friend.

Ginger, you see, is my childhood. Its scent trips the wire inside that says, *I am myself at a million ages.* It is my *Ratatouille* moment.

Ginger is a base ingredient that figures prominently in Chinese cooking; inasmuch as a flavor can be tied to cultural identity, ginger, to me, means Chinese. I am the first generation in my family to be born in America. Am I Chinese? American? Chinese American? In any conversation about race and identity, there are so many complicated threads woven in, so many explainers and disclaimers, that original meaning and intent are often corrupted and lost. But

ginger is an uncomplicated way to feel that identity. It is a pure sensory experience, and it is liberating.

When I miss my mother, I can toss a handful of ginger and baby bok choy into a hot pan, stir-fry it, and be at home in New York with her in five minutes. When I have a sore throat and it's cold outside, I can pour boiling water over a few generous slivers of fresh ginger, add honey, and cradle the mug in my hands. I am back in my grandmother's kitchen, surrounded by my aunties chattering away in Cantonese, and I feel whole.

Ginger, then, is unburdened by what the outside world piles on. It connects me to my family and my past selves. Ginger is a thing I've always loved. Its rough, knobby exterior conceals a heart of gold.

Jen Castle & Blake Spalding

IN 1997, Blake Spalding and Jen Castle were both river chefs, cooking on guided trips in the Grand Canyon. They met at a party, over a food table. Having worked in the food industry for many years, they were both fed up with its patriarchal hierarchy and dreamed of creating a restaurant entirely on their own terms. In 1999, they were invited to open a restaurant where another had closed. The place was called Hell's Backbone Grill, in the remote town of Boulder, Utah, near the boundary of the Grand Staircase–Escalante National Monument—an area of unparalleled landscapes and wildlife that had been designated a national monument three years earlier. With the help of friends, Castle and Spalding scraped together enough money to open the restaurant.

The friends had both traveled extensively, so they understood the comfort of being warmly received while on a journey and wanted to create that experience for others— a sentiment that is essential to their Buddhist-centered mission to be a source of goodness in the world. "Because of our work in the Grand Canyon, we knew the magic and power of an extraordinary landscape and a lovingly prepared meal," says Spalding. Hell's Backbone Grill was perfectly positioned to welcome visitors as they ventured into the wilderness and receive them when they returned, allowing them the opportunity to enjoy an organic, homemade meal along the way.

Equally important to Castle's and Spalding's work is their nearby organic farm, Blaker's Acres, which provides the restaurant with an abundance of seasonal produce. They also source fruit from Boulder's lush heirloom orchards and pasture-raised meat from local ranchers who practice carbon sequestration. These intentional choices are evident in every dish

ABOVE

Hell's Backbone
Grill, adorned in
Tibetan prayer
flags within a
frame of juniper
berries, a local
wild plant

on their menus, like sagebrush-fed lamb with juniper berries and farm kale salad with beehive cheddar, chile almonds, and blackberries.

As young women co-owners and co-chefs in a conservative western outpost, Castle and Spalding worked hard to enmesh themselves in the intimate community of 225 residents. They elicited eye rolls and raised eyebrows at first, but this just galvanized their vision. Hell's Backbone Grill has flourished for more than twenty years, drawing an eclectic crowd of wilderness buffs, foodies, and motorcycle groups, as well as critics' praise.

Fierce collaborators, Castle and Spalding are equal partners in the restaurant; they have no outside investors, which allows them to be nimble as their needs and goals evolve. They have changed lives as well as the local economy: Hell's Backbone operates seven days a week for nine months of the year, and Castle and Spalding are often spread thin between working at the restaurant and the farm and managing their

fifty employees (they are one of the largest employers in the county). Over the past two decades, they have become friends with these employees as well as with their guests. "A lot of people met working here and had babies. It's humbling and tender to think about how much life has happened here," Spalding reflects.

In 2017, they found themselves at the center of a highly politicized battle to protect the Grand Staircase–Escalante National Monument. President Donald Trump had ordered the size of the monument to be cut in half, opening up the land to private mineral extraction and drilling—a threat to the life and community Castle and Spalding have built and the landscape they love. In the months following the administration's announcement, the duo joined a

nonprofit organization in filing a lawsuit against the president and began fundraising for land conservation and rallying support for the cause.

For Castle and Spalding, growing and cooking food are visceral, place-based rituals, as well as moral and political acts. Everything about their complex venture begins and ends with the land: survival, process, communion with nature, conservation, and community. Even in the face of uncertainty and shifting political winds, they continue to abide by the same tenets that compelled them to take a chance years ago. "We are very committed to being a beacon of hope and light," Spalding says. "We like to tell our customers that we are a remote outpost of the resistance. They can feel safe here."

Work Wives

Why is collaboration important to you, and what have you learned from collaborating with each other?

"We're called Pineapple Collaborative for a reason—it truly takes a village to create this multifaceted brand. We always say that we're like peanut butter and jelly: We're better together, and when we fuse our complementary temperaments and skills, we're truly unstoppable. Building a business has been the juggling act of our careers, and the fact that we have each other to share the load makes it so much more enjoyable and manageable."

—**Ariel Pasternak** (CEO)
& Atara Bernstein
cofounders of Pineapple Collaborative
Washington, DC

"Collaboration is a way to strengthen ourselves as well as each other. We've learned the critical value of listening, valuing others' opinions, hearing concerns even when they don't match ours, considering other ways of tackling problems, and simply shouldering the weight of concerns and celebrating the joy of accomplishments with another. We support one another physically, emotionally, and mentally."

—**Rohani Foulkes** (owner) **& Kiki Louya**
cofounders of Folk, Mink, and The Farmer's Hand
Detroit, MI

"We believe in feedback and editing, and when collaborators trust each other, this can be a powerful combination for creating. We learn new things from each other—and also with each other—all the time, and something we've been talking about lately is trusting our gut. Sometimes we need to remind each other that instinct is as critical a component of decision-making as data is. If we didn't have each other, we would likely fall into creative ruts."

—**Merrill Stubbs** (president)
& Amanda Hesser (CEO)
cofounders of Food52
New York, NY

Julia: "As entrepreneurs, our inclination is to have a hand in everything business-related, but I think it's important to identify our weaknesses and partner with people whom we can trust to participate and execute at the same level we would. Collaboration also allows for creativity and growth to happen in a way that they couldn't if there was only one voice involved."

Allie: "It is so helpful to bounce ideas off someone and to know that you aren't alone in taking big risks. It really enables you to put yourself out there and push boundaries."

—**Julia Sullivan** (chef and owner) **& Allie Balin**
cofounders of Henrietta Red
Nashville, TN

"What keeps us interested in our work is our independence. The fact that it's just the two of us making decisions, with the help and input of our staff and managers, means we can be nimble and ethical, while also taking more risks."

—**Jen Castle & Blake Spalding**
co-chefs and co-owners of Hell's Backbone Grill
Boulder, UT

Fill in the blank: "My favorite thing about working with ＿＿＿＿＿ is ＿＿＿＿＿."

Kiki: "My favorite thing about working with Rohani is her unwillingness to give up, even when the cards are seemingly stacked against our favor. She is often the one who reminds me that we can accomplish anything we put our minds to."

Rohani: "My favorite thing about working with Kiki is her endless and uplifting optimism. Also, sometimes she sings to me when she's trying to tell me something."

—**Rohani Foulkes** (owner) **& Kiki Louya**
cofounders of Folk, Mink, and The Farmer's Hand
Detroit, MI

Merrill: "My favorite thing about working with Amanda is that her creative spark and unwavering conviction inspire me to carve out more space for creative, ambitious thinking."

Amanda: "My favorite thing about working with Merrill is her unmatched memory and ability to synthesize a ton of information and express it palatably and concisely. Another favorite—and no less important—thing about working with Merrill is how much more I laugh when she's nearby."

—**Merrill Stubbs** (president)
& Amanda Hesser (CEO)
cofounders of Food52
New York, NY

Julia: "My favorite thing about working with Allie is the way she faces challenging situations. Whether it's a dissatisfied guest or disgruntled employee, she handles things head-on with compassion. Her passion for wine also keeps our list fresh and interesting, which is a great match for our seasonal menu changes."

Allie: "My favorite thing about working with Julia is being inspired by her fearlessness and drive."

—**Julia Sullivan** (chef and owner)
& Allie Balin
cofounders of Henrietta Red
Nashville, TN

Ariel: "My favorite thing about working with Atara is the empathy she has for our community, our team, and me. Business is all about people and relationships, and being attuned to others' emotions and meeting them where they're at is a very special skill and one she has in spades."

Atara: "My favorite thing about working with Ariel is the way she carefully approaches every situation. She's extremely deliberate, always thinking about potential outcomes. She's an incredibly thoughtful person and that shows in how she treats our team, our panelists, and our community."

—**Ariel Pasternak** (CEO)
& Atara Bernstein
cofounders of Pineapple Collaborative
Washington, DC

"Food connects and unites us. It can be both deeply optimistic and reassuring. I believe there is power and healing in inviting everyone into the kitchen."

—Annie Happel
cook and writer

Ashleigh Shanti

VIRGINIA NATIVE Ashleigh Shanti has been a driving force behind Benne on Eagle, a restaurant in Asheville, North Carolina, that opened in 2018. Located in a historically African American neighborhood called the Block, the restaurant honors and explores African American and West African culinary traditions that once thrived in Asheville and throughout Appalachia. As chef de cuisine, Shanti excavates meaningful ingredients (such as the restaurant's namesake benne seed, a relative of the sesame seed that was brought to the United States from West Africa and was commonly grown in the hidden gardens of the enslaved in the 1700s), recipes, and techniques, paying homage to African Americans' integral role in the region's gastronomy and development. In doing so, Shanti creates menus that draw on the Ghanaian concept of sankofa—creating something new while honoring ancestors and past traditions—and celebrate the inextricable link between African American culinary tradition, Appalachia, and her identity.

Cabbage and Wild Mushroom Pancake
with Sauce Affrilachia

Makes 4 pancakes

When I was growing up, my mom would make these delicate, crispy cabbage pancakes for breakfast on the weekends. She'd bulk them up with whatever she could find in the pantry and fridge—spring peas, scallions, bell peppers, canned salmon—and serve them over a bowl of hot grits, just like her own mother would.

Ever the imaginative only child, I'd tightly close my eyes and consume these little delights, pretending I was in front of a teppanyaki grill in Osaka, Japan, munching on okonomiyaki, the konamon (flour-based) dish my dad would often wax poetic about after having lived on the savory street snack for months during his time there. Utilizing the abundance of Asheville's wild mushrooms and the bright boldness of radicchio, this cornmeal pancake recipe pays homage to those highly whimsical moments.

❶ In a small bowl, combine the flour, cornmeal, sugar, and baking powder. Set aside. In a large bowl, beat the eggs and miso into the buttermilk.

❷ Add the dry ingredients to the buttermilk mixture and whisk together to combine.

❸ Add the cabbage, radicchio, and mushrooms to the pancake batter. Toss to combine.

❹ Heat 1 tablespoon of the grapeseed oil over medium heat in a small nonstick skillet. Place 1 cup of the cabbage pancake batter in the skillet and carefully press down to ensure the batter makes contact with the bottom of the skillet, all the way to the outer edges. After 5 to 6 minutes, give the pan a wiggle to release the pancake. Now hold your breath in an attempt

¾ cup all-purpose flour

¾ cup finely ground cornmeal

2 teaspoons sugar

1 teaspoon baking powder

2 cups buttermilk

2 large eggs

2 tablespoons miso paste

1 cup thinly sliced cabbage

¾ cup thinly sliced radicchio

1 cup thinly sliced wild mushrooms

4 tablespoons grapeseed oil

Sauce Affrilachia (see recipe on page 200)

to flip the pancake over. Tilt the pan forward and quickly flick your wrist in an upward motion and flip (or simply use a spatula if this all sounds too intense), then cook the second side for another 5 minutes, until the pancake is firm to the touch and golden brown on both sides. Slide the pancake onto a plate and serve. Repeat with the remaining oil and batter. Serve with Sauce Affrilachia.

Sauce Affrilachia

Makes 1 cup

Combine all the ingredients in a small saucepot and bring to a boil over high heat. Boil for 30 seconds, then reduce the heat to medium-low and cook for 6 minutes (the sauce should coat the back of a spoon).

½ cup apple preserves

½ cup soy sauce

⅛ cup sorghum molasses

4 scallions, thinly sliced

1 tablespoon apple cider vinegar

2 teaspoons ground sumac

1½ teaspoons freshly ground black pepper

1½ teaspoons Dijon mustard

½ teaspoon freshly grated gingerroot

What is the most useful piece of cooking advice you've received?

"You can almost always substitute an ingredient."

—**Tiffany**
Chicago, IL

"I once heard that 'women shouldn't use basil because it's too much of what they already are,' and I can only guess that means intoxicating, strong, seductive, fresh. So I use basil all the damn time in honor of that."

—**Kate**
Mount Desert Island, ME

"I live by the rule that for every recipe, reserve one glass of wine for the cook."

—**Marissa**
Princeton, NJ

"1) Everything needs more salt than you think, and 2) people love to pitch in—ask a friend for help!"

—**Leigha**
San Francisco, CA

"Less is more: Let the food be the food."

—**Wendy**
Grand Rapids, MI

"Let your kids help as much as you can. It builds memories and gives them a life skill."

—**Jenny**
Roanoke, IL

"My mother always told me that your hands are the most useful tool in the kitchen and they are the most washable as well. I use my bare hands to mix doughs and batters, toss salads, and test meat for doneness. "

—**Alice**
Pittsburgh, PA

"Always have a backup plan! Even the best cooks have bad days."

—**Shiloa**
Denham Springs, LA

"Realize that the table is the most important item—good for eating and bonding."

—**Sue**
Fountain Valley, CA

"In college I read Raymond Carver's wonderful short story collections. In the story titled 'A Small, Good Thing,' the narrator says, 'Eating is a small, good thing in a time like this' (the characters are grieving a loss). There is seldom a time when food isn't a small, good gift."

—**Julia**
Richmond, VA

"My mom always said to follow my heart in the kitchen."

—**Mary**
Plainfield, IL

What is the greatest lesson you've learned from cooking?

"Cooking is the universal leveler. No matter what mood you're in, no matter who's at your table or what your beliefs may be, it is the thing that makes us all human, that civilizes us and brings us together."

—Gail Simmons
culinary expert, television personality, cofounder of Bumble Pie Productions, and food writer
New York, NY

"Cooking can change your world, over and over again."

—Rosio Sanchez
chef and owner of Hija de Sanchez and Sanchez Cantina
Copenhagen, Denmark

"The greatest thing I've learned is that passion is key. This is a grueling job, but all of the technical skills can be taught. What we can't teach is passion, which comes from within."

—Barbara Lynch
chef and owner of Barbara Lynch Collective
Boston, MA

"The joy of feeding people. It's the most direct way of expressing love."

—Katie Workman
food writer, recipe developer, and author
New York, NY

"That you have to give respect to get respect. That means respecting the food—where it came from *and* its end result on the plate in front of a guest. That also means respecting your client's needs as well as the people who are working for you."

—Anita Lo
chef, culinary tour guide, and author
New York, NY

"Finding my yummy: discovering how to taste food and feeling empowered by that."

—Carla Hall
chef, television personality, and author
Washington, DC

"One of the greatest things I've learned from cooking is that food is more about the context in which it is created than how it is cooked. Even the most methodical, mundane aspects of cooking become magical when you know why and for whom you are creating food. Your intention goes into every layer of your preparation, from how it's planned to how it lands on your customer's table. Your community feels the love and intention (or the lack thereof) in the food they eat. I try to instill this sense of purpose in every one of my employees, from the dishwasher to the server. The more they understand their role in the experience of a dish, the happier they are."

—Reem Assil
chef and owner of Reem's California,
entrepreneur, and activist
Oakland and San Francisco, CA

"The importance of relationships, history, and culture. What started for me as a simple love of preparing food and feeding others has grown into traveling the world and making lifelong friends while doing it. Every tradition and every dish comes from somewhere and has a story. Through food, I continue to learn about life and people. It's exhilarating when you think about the endless experiences that are still out there to be had."

—Katianna Hong
chef
Los Angeles, CA

Rachel Khong

Rachel Khong is a San Francisco–based writer and author, the former executive editor of Lucky Peach *magazine, and founder of San Francisco's The Ruby, a coworking and gathering space for creative women and nonbinary people that hosts an array of events, including a food and beverage series that celebrates the city's diverse cuisine and features cookbook authors, chefs, and winemakers.*

Fruit

In my family, dessert—in the cake-and-ice-cream sense, anyway—was never a thing. After dinner, my mother would cut fruit for us: slices of apple or pear or melon. Or she'd rinse grapes. She'd lovingly present the fruit on an enamel plate that she also used to steam eggs in the rice cooker. The fruit was always a little bit salty and a little bit garlicky, which we always complained about. She rinsed the apple slices with salt water because, according to her, it would prevent them from browning. And the fruit was reminiscent of garlic because my mom cooked all the time, and her hands permanently smelled like garlic. When I think of my mom, I think of her garlic hands, and I think of fruit.

Once, driving home from a movie theater, where we'd watched *White Fang 2* (my brother and I were suckers for any movie starring a dog), my mother pulled over without a word in front of the Bank of America. I was eight. We lived in a desert town and I remember the day being incredibly hot, dusty. She uncrumpled a plastic bag she kept in the front seat and told us to wait in the car. She started scaling the tree in front of the bank.

"Mom, what are you doing?" my brother and I shouted, mortified.

"They're loquats!" she shouted back, filling her bag. "White people don't know how to eat these!"

When I was twelve, we moved to the house my parents still live in. The house had previously belonged

to a Nigerian American family who had lovingly planted fruit trees in the backyard: grapefruits, lemons, peaches. But their crowning achievement was a giant, majestic fig tree, which every September continues to produce purple figs that we don't eat until they're split and bursting with sweetness. My mother took over the task of tending to these trees, and over the years added her own attempts: apples, oranges, even dragon fruit. She tends to those trees day after day, covering each fruit in mesh and stringing old AOL CDs from the trees' branches to keep birds away. When I'm home, she'll slice her homegrown fruit. Gratefully, now, I'll eat it.

What inspired you to start your ice cream business?

"My parents ran a restaurant for thirty-five years, and I learned everything about food and family in that environment. The ice cream freezer was the place that my siblings and I would always go to create special sundaes when the kitchen wasn't in service. This was our treat and it positioned ice cream as my dessert of choice for the rest of my life. My love for ice cream, the lack of good ice cream in our neighborhood, and the desire to build an inspiring work life in Montana with my husband inspired our business."

—Marissa Keenan
founder of Sweet Peaks Ice Cream
Montana

"Ice cream has been my joy since I can remember. I remember being so small I could just see my granny's knees, and she would take me to Brigham's in Boston.

"Odile Gakire Katese, the Rwandan director who became our partner, said she felt ice cream was the embodiment of an indulgence to which all human beings are entitled. She spoke of her country having been ravaged by the genocide and the need for people to take one moment for themselves and their own enjoyment. It was essential to healing, and without it, a mere life of subsistence was too oppressive to bear. Eating ice cream is a suspended moment of bliss when we step out of the confusion, chaos, depression, stress, pain, helplessness of our regular lives . . . or a way to elevate the warm moments to a deeper positive experience. It is sensual, but innocent. It brings generations together."

—Jennie Dundas
cofounder and CEO of Blue Marble Ice Cream
Brooklyn, NY

"I love how you can create emotion through something as simple as a stroke of pencil or color choice. At some point I fell in love with flavor, which is taste and scent. Ice cream is a nearly blank canvas for flavor and a perfect platform to tell stories and evoke emotion. I made my first batch when I was in art school, and my life was changed forever. I couldn't concentrate on art anymore, so I opened a tiny stand at our farmers market in 1996.

"What I realized is that most ice cream in the United States is nostalgic or backward-looking. As a result, young creative types never thought about ice cream. But I thought I could create a place where my friends would want to hang out. That meant a combination of nostalgia and more challenging, interesting ingredients. And that's what we are still up to today!"

—Jeni Britton Bauer
founder and chief brand officer of
Jeni's Splendid Ice Creams
Columbus, OH

"I majored in architecture and then began to explore the intersection of food and architecture (I call it 'farchitecture') while in grad school. After graduating, I was an architectural intern at Walt Disney's hotel division. I started making ice cream sandwiches and naming the different combinations after famous architects and architectural movements for some comic relief among the staff, since there had been a bunch of recession-based layoffs. During that period, I met Freya Estreller, who is now my wife, and she helped me make those ice cream sandwiches while also crunching the numbers to turn our passionate hobby into an actual business."

—Natasha Case
cofounder and CEO of Coolhaus
Culver City, CA

"While running my first company in Buenos Aires, I fell in love with Argentine-style ice cream; it was decadent, with sophisticated, vibrant, and unusual flavors that seamlessly conveyed a portrait of a grand society. Every block had several ice cream parlors. I loved how ingrained it was in the Argentine lifestyle that it had a culture of its own. At twenty-seven years old, I felt as if it was the first time in my life I had truly experienced ice cream, and that puzzled me. I moved back to Maine with an insatiable desire to learn why Argentine ice cream affected me so differently than the ice creams of my childhood, which fueled me to create this company.

"A year or two into the business, a woman came into the shop, ordered an ice cream, went outside to eat it, and then came back in teary-eyed. She had grown up in Argentina, but her parents sought asylum in New York during the Dirty War and she had never been back. She hugged and thanked me and shared with me beautiful memories of an idyllic childhood spent in Buenos Aires that the ice cream brought back to her. It was the first time in my business I saw the connection between food and memory, and I felt I had succeeded in creating a product that lived up to the standards in Argentina. But more importantly, I realized that my passion had shifted to a desire to create ice cream so others could relive old memories, make new memories, and share experiences."

—Lauren Guptill
founder of Rococo Ice Cream
Kennebunkport, ME

"Ice cream is in my fabric. I can't remember a time when, growing up, our freezer was not stocked with at least two pints of Häagen Dazs. When I was twenty, I found out I had a dairy allergy. I was just about to start culinary school and become a pastry chef, and all I knew was butter and cream. I was distraught, to say the least, that after finally finding my passion, its very ingredients were rejected by my body. And this was 2000 in the suburbs of Seattle, so I didn't know about vegan food yet. So I said fuck it and kept my plans, eating dairy along the way. But I knew that with every bite or drink I was hurting myself inside, so I was constantly feeling guilty and shameful.

"It wasn't until after I started my first company and owned my own dessert restaurant that I started to get sick. I knew I had to stop eating dairy, so I quit. It was incredibly hard to say goodbye to food that I relied on for comfort. After all, it was my career, my livelihood, and deeply rooted in my family. During all of this, I became more and more devastated over the destruction of our natural world and wanted to participate in the future health of our planet. I wanted to figure out a way to make clean vegan ice cream with a more gentle footprint on this earth and without sacrificing anything—the texture, the flavor, the whole experience had to be just as good, if not better, than a dairy ice cream—for people like me, and people with their own reasons, and for Mother Earth, and to hopefully be an inspiration to others."

—Autumn Martin
pastry chef, founder, and
co-owner of Frankie & Jo's
Seattle, WA

Leticia Landa

Leticia Landa is the deputy director of San Francisco's La Cocina, a nonprofit incubator that supports food entrepreneurs as they develop and grow their businesses.

Albóndigas

My mom hides chopped hard-boiled eggs in the center of every meatball she makes. The first time I had classic spaghetti and meatballs, I confusedly asked my friend Sarah, "Where is the egg?" She looked at me like I was a Martian. A Mexican, actually. Since then, I've learned it's not how all Mexicans make them, just how my mom (who is also named Leticia, but goes by Letty) happens to make them, because that's how her mom did it. Unfortunately, we can no longer ask my abuela Josefina why she included chopped eggs, but my guess is that it was my bisabuela Mercedes's doing.

Albóndigas y arroz was in frequent rotation on our dinner table growing up. My parents emigrated from Mexico City to Austin, Texas, just before I was born. My dad came to get his master's degree and then started a software company, while my mom took care of me and my two little sisters. Many of my early memories are in the kitchen; I'd pull up a stool and "help" my mom, who cooked dinner from scratch every night. She told me my little fingers were perfect for making the dent in the albóndigas and reminded me that I had to stand back once we put them in the tomato sauce, in case the sauce jumped out at us. At the time I had no idea, but now I can only imagine how homesick she was. I think she cooked as a way to feel connected to her past, and to connect us to the flavors that she knew we were missing out on as we grew up and started asking for peanut butter and jelly to be rolled up in our tortillas and squishing up our faces when not-that-spicy foods were "too spicy."

this country with, yet kitchen work is incredibly undervalued. Taking those skills and turning them into business ownership gives families assets and economic security that hourly labor rarely can. Using their beloved family recipes to build economic freedom keeps their rich heritage alive.

On the next page is Isabel Caudillo's recipe for albóndigas from the cookbook I cowrote, *We Are La Cocina: Recipes in Pursuit of the American Dream*. Since 2008, I've worked with entrepreneurs from all over the United States and immigrants from as far away as Senegal, Japan, and Malaysia. Isabel is from Mexico City, which is where both of my parents grew up, so I feel a special connection to her and a near-constant craving for the dishes she serves at El Buen Comer, the restaurant she opened in 2017. It's not far from my house, and though they are missing the egg-filled centers, her albóndigas remind me so much of my mom's. I order them every time I stop in and I can't wait for my daughter (who only drinks milk at the moment) to grow to love them as much as I do.

My parents' immigration and my father's establishment of a business completely transformed my life, so ensuring that others have the same opportunity has been the focus of my career. I think of my mom and grandmothers often while I'm working at La Cocina. Many of the people I work with are immigrants, and like my mom, they've had to adapt to new circumstances and new ingredients while maintaining the heart of each of the dishes they grew up with. Kitchen skills are something many women arrive in

ABOVE

Landa's Otomí tablecloth, a wedding gift from her grandmother's best friend

Isabel Caudillo's Albóndigas

Makes 20 to 30 meatballs in sauce

1 Make the meatballs: In a food processor, pulse the onion, garlic, and mint until very finely chopped. Transfer this mixture to a large bowl and combine with the eggs. Add the ground beef and the salt. Combine, using your hands.

Using an ice cream scoop or a tablespoon, measure out 1½ to 2 tablespoons of the mixture per ball (about 2 ounces each). In a large Dutch oven, heat a tablespoon of oil over medium-high heat. Brown the meatballs in batches, turning occasionally, 6 to 8 minutes per batch, adding oil as needed.

2 Meanwhile, make the sauce: Combine the tomatoes, chipotles, onion, garlic, oil, salt, and ½ cup water in a blender and pulse until it forms a smooth purée. Drain all but 2 tablespoons of the fat from the Dutch oven and heat over medium-high, then add the tomato-chipotle purée. Turn the heat to low and simmer for about 6 minutes. Taste and add more salt if needed. Add the meatballs and gently coat them with sauce. Cover and let simmer until the meatballs are cooked all the way through, about 15 minutes. Serve with the rice and beans.

MEATBALLS

½ small onion, roughly chopped

2 cloves garlic

¼ cup fresh mint leaves

2 large eggs

2 pounds lean ground beef

2 teaspoons kosher salt

Canola oil, for frying

SAUCE

12 medium Roma tomatoes, quartered

3 chipotles in adobo sauce

½ small onion, roughly chopped

2 cloves garlic

1 tablespoon canola oil

1 teaspoon kosher salt, plus extra as needed

Rice and beans, for serving

LANDA FAMILY EGG MODIFICATION

When you start to make the meatballs, boil a few eggs, then peel and dice them. Roll a meatball, then push your thumb into the middle. Fill the indentation with egg, pinch the meat over the hole, and re-roll. Once you've filled all of the meatballs, boil them in the sauce. Serve them over rice with warm corn tortillas on the side. Or over spaghetti, if that's more your thing.

Recipe adapted from *We Are La Cocina* by Leticia Landa and Caleb Zigas. Text copyright © 2019 by La Cocina. Used by permission of Chronicle Books. All rights reserved.

How do conversations about food inspire you?

"A friendship that has food and cooking at the core deepens through that lens. We send each other recipes, we bring each other dishes we know the other will enjoy, we comfort by knowing what the other will savor. Food takes us all over the place, from the kitchen counter to the dinner table to the restaurant bar to far-off lands: a shared quest of flavor and connection."

—Kate
Mount Desert Island, ME

"I LOVE eating! My husband and I often talk about what we (more he) are going to make. He is always willing to try something new, so I experience the joy of finding new recipes and then he gets joy from trying to make them."

—Heather
New York, NY

"It's the joy of the warm and lively gathering of family and friends that inspires me to try new recipes and to create a feast for the eyes and the palate."

—Laurie
Grand Rapids, MI

"My mother and I used to have regular phone calls to talk about our 'food porn' selections. We were supposed to each pick one recipe from *Bon Appétit* every month and then cook both selections, but usually we would get on the phone not having made our choices and go through the magazine together, looking at all the recipes we had earmarked. It was like we were in the kitchen together sharing an experience, more than just updating each other on our lives apart from one another."

—Sommerville
Birmingham, AL

"My girlfriends and I share healthy and fresh recipes on the weekly. It's another way to stay connected."

—Sara
Boston, MA

"I love planning elaborate meals with my brother. He is an amazing cook, he is creative and inventive, and best of all, he is patient! His enthusiasm rubs off on me, and we usually end up picking incredibly complicated recipes to make together."

—Hannah
Montpelier, VT

"I have a dear friend who is an amazing cook and amazingly generous. At particularly busy or sick times, she drops by with meals ready to go. I truly believe there is nothing nicer than the gift of food. She inspires me to give that to others."

—Jeanne
Hinsdale, IL

"My friends and I started an 'international breakfast club' where every month we take turns cooking and sharing food from our cultural traditions (Taiwanese, Indian, and Mexican). Five years later, we've also experimented with many other cultural traditions and food from places of travel. It started with one couple and two friends, and now we are three couples with two babies and one more on the way. The supportive, lighthearted, and experimental nature of our get-togethers inspires me to try new things and dig into my roots."

—Pei-Ru
San Francisco, CA

"Cooking makes me feel connected to my dad. Every time we make something, my girls like to call and tell him about it. He clips recipes out of magazines and mails them to me, and I email links to him. I love connecting with him through cooking."

—Sarah
New York, NY

"Cooking can change your world, over and over again."

—Rosio Sanchez
chef and owner of Hija de Sanchez
and Sanchez Cantina

Haile Thomas

WHEN HAILE THOMAS was eight years old, her father was diagnosed with type 2 diabetes. After researching alternative therapies, Thomas's family decided to make dramatic changes to their diet and lifestyle and prioritized healthy eating. Within a year, they saw notable improvements in her father's condition without using medication.

The experience was a defining moment in Thomas's young life. Her curiosity about cooking, food, and wellness bloomed; she soaked up everything she could learn about nutrition and the importance of conscious eating. As an elementary school student in Tucson, Arizona, she was also aware of the lack of nutrition education among her peers. Her newly acquired knowledge was empowering, and with her parents' encouragement, she began hosting cooking demonstrations and speaking publicly about wellness and nutrition to youth groups in community centers, schools, and summer camps in her hometown.

At the age of twelve, bolstered by the firm belief that "young people should not only be educated, but also be leaders in their lives when it comes to health and well-being," Thomas and her mother cofounded a nonprofit organization called Healthy Active Positive Purposeful Youth (HAPPY). They partnered with a local YMCA to provide free holistic health education to kids in underserved communities. Their story quickly gained national attention, and not long after, Thomas was honored by First Lady Michelle Obama for her leadership in helping kids embrace healthful eating habits.

Thomas credits her parents with creating a supportive foundation and learning environment that inspired her to give back. "This

> "I love teaching and being able to see the kids' reactions to and experiences with the food and recipes that we make. Nothing is more fulfilling than seeing that connection happen."

was sparked from something so simple and something that happens within so many families every day. I think that in itself speaks to the power of our personal journeys and taking that one extra step to share it with others," she says. She enthusiastically embraces the power of technology to spread her empowering message on her podcast, cooking show, and social media.

In 2016, her family relocated to upstate New York to expand HAPPY's programming and impact a larger population, and a year later, Thomas became the youngest certified integrative nutrition coach in the United States. When asked what the future might hold,

Thomas expresses interest in someday studying nutrigenomics, the interaction of nutrition and genes and its relationship to treating disease. But for now, she's fully invested in her many passions: holistic wellness, traveling, farming, youth empowerment, and social justice, to name a few.

"All of these topics hold a special place in my heart because they are interconnected. Oftentimes we try to separate different topics and act like they aren't related, but at the end of the day, they're connected on a systemic level and social level. Until we embrace and talk more about this connectivity and become more inclusive, we cannot get a point across, let alone progress. Period," says Thomas. "But we are the ones who can change the narrative."

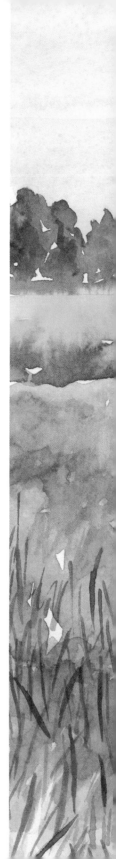

What do you hope will change in the future?

"That our work to create a regenerative food system is directly linked to creating a more just and inclusive society. To meaningfully and honestly deconstruct the structural racism and inequity that divide us along social and economic lines, our communities must show up, listen, cook, organize, and vote."

—Shakirah Simley
director of the Office of Racial Equity for
the City and County of San Francisco
and founder of Nourish | Resist
San Francisco, CA

"I would like to see people taking a different interest in where they're spending their time and money. As a society, we have drawn a lot of lines in the sand—no factory farming, shop local, eat organic, etc.—but when it comes to the social and political practices of our favorite restaurants, the dining community has been surprisingly silent. I would like to see a world where diners care as much about the culture a restaurant creates for its team as they care about which local farm their heirloom tomatoes are coming from."

—Zoe Schor
chef and owner of Split-Rail
and co-owner of Dorothy
Chicago, IL

"Education and recognizing vulnerability are so critical in this industry, which is consistently evolving. It is our obligation to care for and nurture the next generation of cooks and humans, regardless of who they are and where they come from."

—Isabel Coss
pastry chef at Cosme
New York, NY

"For so long, people assumed you had to work in a kitchen to have a career in the food industry. But that seems to be changing, making the culinary conversation much more diverse and compelling. I see an opportunity for me to impact change through the types of stories I tell and the people I feature in my books."

—Julia Sherman
creator of Salad for President and writer
Los Angeles, CA

"I am constantly learning how to grow my business and create a culture, values, and mission statement that push us to make a positive impact on the world. The stakes are higher because there are people who depend on me and the success of our business for their own lives, their families' lives, and their futures. That is a huge responsibility, and I am pushing myself and my teams to set a new standard for benefits and culture in the restaurant industry."

—Katie Button
executive chef and CEO of
Katie Button Restaurants
Asheville, NC

"Right now my goal is to bring in more women of color and create a new table. Primarily, Black women. I identify as a Black woman in wine, and marginalization and racism are prevalent. My continued work is not only getting a seat, but creating a new table."

—Julia Coney
wine writer, educator, consultant,
and founder of Black Wine Professionals
Washington, DC, and Houston, TX

"In Berkeley in the '70s, we were talking about climate change, and it all seemed exaggerated and like we were being really alarmist. It turns out we weren't alarmist enough! I'm glad people are recognizing it now. It's late, but hopefully it's not too late. . . . Climate change is the only thing, ultimately, that really matters. Everything is kind of moot if we don't fix this. And this generation really cares and gets it."

—Ruth Reichl
food writer, editor, and author
Upstate NY

Contributors

For a complete list of awards, visit workman.com/whywecook.

Maryam Ahmed

Consultant, coach, and creator of the Diversity in Wine Leadership Forum

maryamahmed.co

pp. 24, 25, 63

Laurel Almerinda

Pastry chef and director of bakery operations at Huckleberry Bakery & Café and coauthor of *Huckleberry: Stories, Secrets, and Recipes from Our Kitchen*

huckleberrycafe.com

p. 101

Liz Alpern

Creator of Queer Soup Night, co-owner of the Gefilteria, food systems consultant, and coauthor of *The Gefilte Manifesto: New Recipes for Old World Jewish Foods*

queersoupnight.com, gefilteria.com

pp. 120–122

Reem Assil

Chef and owner of Reem's California, entrepreneur, and activist

reem-assil.com, reemscalifornia.com

pp. 34, 62, 128, 177, 203

Sadia Badiei

BSc Dietetics and founder of Pick Up Limes

pickuplimes.com

pp. 158, 159

Allie Balin

Restaurant consultant, sommelier, and cofounder of Henrietta Red

alliebalin.com

pp. 149, 195, 196

Jeni Britton Bauer

Founder and chief brand officer of Jeni's Splendid Ice Creams and author of *Jeni's Splendid Ice Creams at Home* and *Jeni's Splendid Ice Cream Desserts*

jenis.com

p. 207

Minara Begum

Cocreator of Bandhu Gardens, community organizer, chef, mother, and gardener

bandhugardens.com

pp. 106–108

Abra Berens

Chef at Granor Farm and author of *Ruffage: A Practical Guide to Vegetables*

abraberens.com, granorfarm.com

pp. 26–27, 158, 159

Atara Bernstein

Cofounder of Pineapple Collaborative

pineapplecollaborative.com

pp. 194, 196

Elizabeth Binder

Chef and owner of Hand-Crafted Catering

elizabethbinder.com

pp. 102–103

Susan Sokol Blosser

Founder of Sokol Blosser Winery and author of four books

sokolblosser.com

p. 135

Maya-Camille Broussard

Chef and owner of Justice of the Pies

justiceofthepies.com

pp. 100, 101

Elaine Chukan Brown

Wine writer, philosopher, illustrator, and speaker

wakawakawinereviews.com

pp. 171–173

Katie Button

Executive chef and CEO of Katie Button Restaurants, Cúrate Bar de Tapas, and La Bodega by Cúrate and author of *Cúrate: Authentic Spanish Food from an American Kitchen*

katiebuttonrestaurants.com

pp. 75, 95, 221

Natasha Case

Cofounder and CEO of Coolhaus

cool.haus

p. 207

Jen Castle

Co-chef and co-owner of Hell's Backbone Grill, environmental activist, and coauthor of *This Immeasurable Place: Food and Farming from the Edge of Wilderness* and *With a Measure of Grace: The Story and Recipes of a Small Town Restaurant*

hellsbackbonegrill.com

pp. 190–193, 195

Gray Chapman

Journalist

graywrites.com

Christa Chase

Chef at Friends and Family

friendsandfamilybar.com

Polina Chesnakova

Food writer, cooking instructor, and author of *Hot Cheese: Over 50 Gooey, Oozy, Melty Recipes*

chesnokblog.com

Amanda Cohen

Chef and owner of Dirt Candy and author of *The Dirt Candy Cookbook: Flavor-Forward Food from the Upstart New York City Vegetarian Restaurant*

dirtcandynyc.com

Julia Coney

Wine writer, educator, consultant, and founder of Black Wine Professionals

juliaconey.com, blackwineprofessionals.com

Isabel Coss

Pastry chef at Cosme

cosmenyc.com

Ana Diogo-Draper

Director of winemaking at Artesa Vineyards & Winery

artesawinery.com

Jennie Dundas

Cofounder and CEO of Blue Marble Ice Cream

bluemarbleicecream.com

Hillel Echo-Hawk

Chef and owner of Birch Basket Catering, Indigenous food sovereignty activist, member of I-Collective, and speaker

icollective.org

Roz Edison

Cofounder and COO of Marination

marinationmobile.com

Osayi Endolyn

Writer, editor, and media commentator

osayiendolyn.com

Renee Erickson

Chef and co-owner of Sea Creatures restaurants and coauthor of *A Boat, a Whale & a Walrus: Menus and Stories*

reneeerickson.com, eatseacreatures.com

Kristen Essig

Co-chef and co-owner of Coquette and Thalia

coquettenola.com, thalianola.com

Anya Fernald

Cofounder and CEO of Belcampo Meat Company and author of *Home Cooked: Essential Recipes for a New Way to Cook*

belcampo.com

Ikeisha Fields

Chef and owner of Soul Skillet Street Kitchen

soulskillet.com

Robyn Sue Fisher

Founder, CEO, and Chief Brrrista of Smitten Ice Cream

smittenicecream.com

Sara Forte

Writer, creator of the *Sprouted Kitchen* blog and Sprouted Kitchen Cooking Club, and author of *The Sprouted Kitchen: A Tastier Take on Whole Foods* and *Sprouted Kitchen: Bowl + Spoon*

sproutedkitchen.cc

Rohani Foulkes

She/her/hers, Indigenous, First Nation Australian, US immigrant, chef, educator, cofounder and owner of The Farmer's Hand, Folk, and Mink, and managing partner of Nest Egg Hospitality Group

folkdetroit.com, minkdetroit.com

Abby Fuller

Documentary filmmaker and cofounder of A Perfect Day Farm

abby-fuller.com, apdfarm.com

pp. 46–49

Angela Garbacz

Pastry chef and owner of Goldenrod Pastries, founder of Empower Through Flour, and author of *Perfectly Golden: Adaptable Recipes for Sweet and Simple Treats*

goldenrodpastries.com, empowerthroughflour.com

pp. 63, 100, 101

Anna Francese Gass

Chef, recipe tester, food writer, and author of *Heirloom Kitchen: Heritage Recipes and Family Stories from the Tables of Immigrant Women*

annasheirloomkitchen.com

pp. 95, 129, 187

Caroline Glover

Chef and founder of Annette

annettescratchtotable.com

pp. 38, 129

Joyce Goldstein

Chef, restaurant consultant, founding member of Women Chefs and Restaurateurs, teacher, lecturer, and author of twenty-eight cookbooks

joycegoldstein.com

pp. 110–111, 166

Bryony Grealish

Founder and owner of the Fingerless Kitchen, cooking show host, and speaker

thefingerlesskitchen.com

pp. 24, 25

Dorie Greenspan

Writer, *New York Times Magazine* columnist, and author of thirteen cookbooks

doriegreenspan.com

pp. 29, 44–45, 104

Lauren Guptill

Founder of Rococo Ice Cream

rococoicecream.com

p. 208

Christine Ha

Chef and co-owner of the Blind Goat and Xin Chào and author of *Recipes from My Home Kitchen: Asian and American Comfort Food*

theblindcook.com, theblindgoat.com, xinchaohtx.com

pp. 145–147

Carla Hall

Chef, television personality, culinary ambassador for Sweet Home Café at the Smithsonian National Museum of African American History and Culture, and author of three cookbooks

carlahall.com

pp. 8–9, 128, 202

Annie Happel

Cook and writer

happeltree.com

pp. 154–155, 197

Deborah A. Harris

Professor of sociology at Texas State University and coauthor of *Taking the Heat: Women Chefs and Gender Inequality in the Professional Kitchen*

pp. 82–83

Jessica B. Harris

Culinary historian, professor emerita at Queens College, City University of New York, journalist, conceptualizing consultant for Sweet Home Café at the Smithsonian National Museum of African American History and Culture, founding member of the Southern Foodways Alliance, speaker, consultant, and editor, author, or translator of eighteen books

africooks.com

pp. 64–66, 176, 187

Amanda Hesser

Cofounder and CEO of Food52, writer, editor, and author/coauthor of seven books

food52.com

pp. 194, 196

Tanya Holland

Chef and owner of Brown Sugar Kitchen, television personality, speaker, and author of *Brown Sugar Kitchen: New-Style, Down-Home Recipes from Sweet West Oakland* and *New Soul Cooking: Updating a Cuisine Rich in Flavor and Tradition*

tanyaholland.com

pp. 38, 140–141

Katianna Hong

Chef

pp. 29, 39, 96–99, 203

Martha Hoover

Restaurateur and founder of Patachou Inc. and the Patachou Foundation

patachouinc.com, thepatachoufoundation.org

pp. 24, 25, 186

Andréa McBride John

CEO, vintner, and sister of McBride Sisters Wine Collection

mcbridesisters.com

pp. 134, 177

Arielle Johnson

Flavor scientist, writer, and science officer on Food Network's *Good Eats*

ariellejohnson.com

pp. 137–139

Marissa Keenan

Founder of Sweet Peaks Ice Cream

sweetpeaksicecream.com

p. 206

Rachel Khong

Writer, founder of the Ruby, and author of *Goodbye, Vitamin*

rachelkhong.com, therubysf.com

pp. 204–205

Samantha Klimaszewski

Co-chef and co-owner of Lumpia City

lumpiacity.com

pp. 70, 71

Yewande Komolafe

Writer, recipe developer, food stylist, owner of Four Salt Spoons, and creator of My Immigrant Food Is . . .

yewandekomolafe.com

pp. 35–37

Priya Krishna

Writer and author of *Indian-Ish: Recipes and Antics from a Modern American Family*

priyakrishna.me

pp. 12–14, 176

Cheetie Kumar

Chef and owner of Garland, Neptunes Parlour, and Kings and guitarist in the band Birds of Avalon

garlandraleigh.com, kingsraleigh.com

pp. 28, 94, 128

Leticia Landa

Deputy director of La Cocina and coauthor of *We Are La Cocina: Recipes in Pursuit of the American Dream*

lacocinasf.org

pp. 210–213

Irene Li

Chef and owner of Mei Mei Restaurant, sustainability and social justice activist, and coauthor of *Double Awesome Chinese Food: Irresistible and Totally Achievable Recipes from Our Chinese-American Kitchen*

meimeiboston.com

pp. 63, 70, 71, 93, 94, 104

Jodi Liano

Founder and director of San Francisco Cooking School, cooking instructor, writer, and author of six cookbooks

sfcooking.com

pp. 62, 149, 167

Anita Lo

Chef, culinary tour guide, and author of *Cooking Without Borders* and *Solo: A Modern Cookbook for a Party of One*

chefanitalo.com

pp. 38, 75, 88–89, 186, 202

Jane Lopes

Sommelier, cofounder of LEGEND Wine Imports, and author of *Vignette: Stories of Life and Wine in 100 Bottles*

janelopes.com, legendaustralia.com

pp. 63, 136

Kiki Louya

Chef, entrepreneur, food systems activist, speaker, and cofounder of Folk, The Farmer's Hand, and Nest Egg Hospitality Group

kikilouya.com

pp. 194, 195

Lisa Ludwinski

Chef and owner of Sister Pie and author of *Sister Pie: The Recipes and Stories of a Big-Hearted Bakery in Detroit*

sisterpie.com

pp. 100, 101

Barbara Lynch

Chef and owner of Barbara Lynch Collective and author of *Out of Line: A Life of Playing with Fire* and *Stir: Mixing It Up in the Italian Tradition*

barbaralynch.com

pp. 76–77, 167, 177, 202

Deborah Madison

Chef, cooking teacher, master gardener, writer, and author of fourteen cookbooks and a memoir

deborahmadison.com

pp. 95, 159, 160–161

Cara Mangini

Restaurateur, chef, and author of *The Vegetable Butcher: How to Select, Prep, Slice, Dice, and Masterfully Cook Vegetables from Artichokes to Zucchini*

thevegetablebutcher.com

pp. 178–181

Autumn Martin

Pastry chef, founder, and co-owner of Frankie & Jo's, founder and owner of Hot Cakes, and author of *Malts & Milkshakes: 60 Recipes for Frosty, Creamy Frozen Treats*

frankieandjos.com, getyourhotcakes.com

p. 209

Cristina Martinez

Chef and co-owner of South Philly Barbacoa and Casa Mexico and cofounder of Popular Alliance for Undocumented Workers' Rights

casamexicophilly.com

pp. 72–74

Robin McBride

President, vintner, and sister of McBride Sisters Wine Collection

mcbridesisters.com

pp. 134, 177

Mimi Mendoza

Pastry chef at Senia

restaurantsenia.com

pp. 28, 75, 123–125, 166, 176

Preeti Mistry

Chef, entrepreneur, speaker, activist, and coauthor of *The Juhu Beachclub Cookbook: Indian Spice, Oakland Soul*

pp. 28, 62, 149

Niki Nakayama

Chef and owner of n/naka

n-naka.com

pp. 162–165, 177

Alana Newhouse

Writer, founder and editor in chief of *Tablet* magazine, and author of *The 100 Most Jewish Foods: A Highly Debatable List* and *The Passover Haggadah: An Ancient Story for Modern Times*

tabletmag.com

pp. 150–151

Ariel Pasternak

Cofounder and CEO of Pineapple Collaborative

pineapplecollaborative.com

pp. 194, 196

Jen Pelka

Cofounder of Une Femme Wines and founder and CEO of Magnum PR

unefemmewines.com, magnumpr.co

p. 134

Leah Penniman

Cofounder, co-executive director, and farm manager of Soul Fire Farm, educator, food justice activist, and author of *Farming While Black: Soul Fire Farm's Practical Guide to Liberation on the Land*

soulfirefarm.org

pp. 20–22, 148

Nicole Ponseca

Restaurateur, founder and creative director of Jeepney, speaker, and coauthor of *I Am a Filipino: And This Is How We Cook*

jeepneynyc.com

pp. 42–43

Rose Previte

Restaurateur and owner of Maydān and Compass Rose

maydandc.com, compassrosedc.com

pp. 28, 166

Amy Quichiz

Founder of Veggie Mijas, writer, and activist

veggiemijas.com

pp. 25, 158, 177

Ruth Reichl

Food writer, editor, speaker, and author of five memoirs, a novel, and two cookbooks

ruthreichl.com

pp. 4–7, 221

Alexa Reyes

Co-chef and co-owner of Lumpia City

lumpiacity.com

pp. 70, 71

June Rodil

Master sommelier, partner at Goodnight Hospitality and June's All Day, and creator of June Brut Rosé

goodnighthospitality.com, junesallday.com

pp. 63, 135

Ashley Rodriguez

Cook, cocreator, host, and coproducer of *Kitchen Unnecessary*, writer, and author of *Date Night In: More Than 120 Recipes to Nourish Your Relationship* and *Let's Stay In: More Than 120 Recipes to Nourish the Ones You Love*

notwithoutsalt.com, kitchenunnecessary.com

pp. 168–169

Ana Roš

Chef and co-owner of Hiša Franko and author of *Ana Roš: Sun and Rain*

hisafranko.com

pp. 30–31

Amanda Saab

Cocreator of Dinner with Your Muslim Neighbor and blogger at Amanda's Plate

amandasplate.com

pp. 52–54

Celia Sack

Rare books specialist and owner of Omnivore Books

omnivorebooks.com

pp. 40–41

Jordan Salcito

Sommelier, founder of Ramona and Bellus Wines, director of Wine Special Projects at Momofuku, and entrepreneur

drinkramona.com, belluswines.com

p. 136

Rosio Sanchez

Chef and owner of Hija de Sanchez and Sanchez Cantina

hijadesanchez.dk, lovesanchez.com

pp. 55–57, 186, 202, 216

Kamala Saxton

Cofounder of Marination, Super Six, and Good Bar

marinationmobile.com, supersixseattle.com, goodbarseattle.com

pp. 70, 71

Zoe Schor

Chef and owner of Split-Rail and co-owner of Dorothy

splitrailchicago.com

pp. 94, 129, 220

Ashleigh Shanti

Chef de cuisine at Benne on Eagle

benneoneagle.com

pp. 198–200

Julia Sherman

Creator of Salad for President, writer, and author of *Salad for President: A Cookbook Inspired by Artists*

saladforpresident.com

pp. 158, 159, 221

Siska Silitonga

Chef and owner of ChiliCali

chilicali.com

pp. 70, 71

Shakirah Simley

Director of the Office of Racial Equity for the City and County of San Francisco, founder of Nourish | Resist, food justice activist, writer, and community organizer

shakirahsimley.com, nourishresist.org

pp. 24, 149, 220

Gail Simmons

Culinary expert, television personality, cofounder of Bumble Pie Productions, food writer, and author of *Talking with My Mouth Full: My Life as a Professional Eater* and *Bringing it Home: Favorite Recipes from a Life of Adventurous Eating*

gailsimmons.com

pp. 148, 174–175, 202

Mutsuko Soma

Chef, sake sommelier, and owner of Kamonegi and Hannyatou

kamonegiseattle.com, hannyatou.com

pp. 182–185

Blake Spalding

Co-chef and co-owner of Hell's Backbone Grill, environmental activist, and coauthor of *This Immeasurable Place: Food and Farming from the Edge of Wilderness* and *With a Measure of Grace: The Story and Recipes of a Small Town Restaurant*

hellsbackbonegrill.com

pp. 190–193, 195

Stevie Stacionis

Sommelier, co-owner of MAMA Oakland and Bay Grape, and founder of Bâtonnage Forum

mama-oakland.com, baygrapewine.com, batonnageforum.com

p. 136

Emily Staugaitis

Cocreator of Bandhu Gardens, community organizer, and gardener

bandhugardens.com

pp. 106–108

Merrill Stubbs

Cofounder and president of Food52, writer, and coauthor of three books

food52.com

pp. 194, 196

Julia Sullivan

Chef, cofounder, and owner of Henrietta Red

henriettared.com

pp. 148, 195, 196

Haile Thomas

Founder and CEO of HAPPY, activist, certified integrative health and nutrition coach, speaker, and author of *Living Lively: 80 Plant Based Recipes to Activate Your Power & Feed Your Potential*

hailevthomas.com

pp. 217–219

Jess Thomson

Writer, recipe developer, and author/coauthor of ten cookbooks and a memoir

jessthomsonwrites.com

pp. 90–92

Bonnie Tsui

Journalist, founding member of La Cocina's *F&B: Voices from the Kitchen*, and author of *Why We Swim* and *American Chinatown: A People's History of Five Neighborhoods*

bonnietsui.com, voicesfromthekitchen.org

pp. 188–189

Julia Turshen

Cook, food writer, speaker, founder of Equity at the Table, author of three cookbooks, and coauthor of numerous cookbooks

juliaturshen.com, equityatthetable.com

pp. 18–19

Kate Williams

Chef and owner of Lady of the House, Karl's, and Candy Bar

ladyofthehousedetroit.com, karlsdetroit.com, candybardetroit.com

pp. 130–132

Katie Workman

Food writer, recipe developer, cohost of *Real Life Kitchen*, and author of *Dinner Solved: 100 Ingenious Recipes That Make the Whole Family Happy, Including You!* and *The Mom 100 Cookbook: 100 Recipes Every Mom Needs in Her Back Pocket*

themom100.com

pp. 75, 202

Nite Yun

Chef and owner of Nyum Bai

nyumbai.com

pp. 156–157

Credits

Contributor Copyrights

Essay (pp. 4–7) copyright © 2021 by Ruth Reichl

Essay (pp. 15–17) copyright © 2021 by Gray Chapman

Essay (p. 19) copyright © 2021 by Julia Turshen

Recipe (p. 27) copyright © 2021 by Abra Berens

Essay (p. 37) copyright © 2021 by Yewande Komolafe

Essay (pp. 47–49) copyright © 2021 by Abby Fuller

Essay (pp. 53–54) copyright © 2021 by Amanda Saab

Recipe (pp. 65–66) copyright © 2021 by Jessica B. Harris

Essay (pp. 67–69) copyright © 2021 by Amanda Cohen

Recipe (pp. 79–80) copyright © 2021 by Hillel Echo-Hawk

Essay (pp. 82–83) copyright © 2021 by Deborah A. Harris

Essay (pp. 90–92) copyright © 2021 by Jess Thomson

Essay (pp. 97–99) copyright © 2021 by Katianna Hong

Recipe (p. 103) copyright © 2021 by Elizabeth Binder

Essay (pp. 116–118) copyright © 2021 by Osayi Endolyn

Recipe (pp. 124–125) copyright © 2021 by Mimi Mendoza

Essay (pp. 137–139) copyright © 2021 by Arielle Johnson

Recipe (pp. 143–144) copyright © 2021 by Sara Forte

Essay (pp. 150–151) copyright © 2021 by Alana Newhouse

Essay (pp. 154–155) copyright © 2021 by Annie Happel

Recipe (p. 157) copyright © 2021 by Nite Yun

Recipe (p. 169) copyright © 2021 by Ashley Rodriguez

Essay (pp. 171–173) copyright © 2021 by Elaine Chukan Brown

Essay (pp. 178–179) copyright © 2021 by Cara Mangini

Essay (pp. 188–189) copyright © 2021 by Bonnie Tsui

Recipe (pp. 199–200) copyright © 2021 by Ashleigh Shanti

Essay (pp. 204–205) copyright © 2021 by Rachel Khong

Source Images

The following illustrations were based on the sources below, with permission and my gratitude.

Pp. 8–9, Carla Hall: Source photograph by Marvin Joseph/ *The Washington Post* via Getty Images

Pp. 32–33, Renee Erickson: Source photograph by Charity Burggraaf

P. 64, Jessica B. Harris: Source photograph by Rog and Bee Walker

Pp. 72–73, Cristina Martinez: Source photograph by Ted Nghiem

P. 77, Barbara Lynch: Source photograph by Michael Prince

Pp. 88–89, Anita Lo: Source photograph by Doron Gild

P. 106, Minara Begum and Emily Staugaitis: Source photograph by Mark Kurlylandchik for *The Detroit Free Press*

P. 121, Liz Alpern: Source photograph by Aaron Samuel Breslow

P. 131, Parisian ham plate: Source photograph by Marvin Shaoni

Pp. 140–141, Tanya Holland: Source photograph by Smeeta Mahanti

P. 174, Gail Simmons: Source photograph by Kristen Kilpatrick

Quote Sources

P. 23, Jocelyn Jackson: Instagram post (@justuskitchen), June 9, 2020

P. 81, Asma Khan: *Chef's Table* (Netflix), Season 6, Episode 3

P. 119, Samin Nosrat: Susanna Hutcheson, "How I became a chef and writer: Samin Nosrat, author of 'Salt Fat Acid Heat,'" *USA Today*, November 20, 2018

P. 133, Dominique Crenn: *Chef's Table* (Netflix), Season 2, Episode 3

P. 170, Mashama Bailey: *Chef's Table* (Netflix), Season 6, Episode 1

Endnotes

1. Lindsey Smith Taillie, "Who's cooking? Trends in US home food preparation by gender, education, and race/ethnicity from 2003 to 2016," *Nutrition Journal* 17, no. 41 (April 2018), https://doi.org/10.1186/s12937-018-0347-9.

2. Alexis Krivkovich and Marie-Claude Nadeau, *Women in the Food Industry*, McKinsey & Company, November 2017, https://www.mckinsey.com/featured-insights/gender-equality/women-in-the-food-industry.

3. "Chefs and Head Cooks," Data USA, https://www.datausa.io/profile/soc/chefs-head-cooks.

4. Diana Ellsworth, Ana Mendy, and Gavin Sullivan, "How the LGBTQ+ community fares in the workplace," McKinsey & Company, June 23, 2020, https://www.mckinsey.com/featured-insights/diversity-and-inclusion/how-the-lgbtq-plus-community-fares-in-the-workplace.

Rachel Thomas et al., *Women in the Workplace 2019*, Lean In and McKinsey & Company, October 2019, https://wiw-report.s3.amazonaws.com/Women_in_the_Workplace_2019.pdf.

5. Gina Trapani and Matt Jacobs, "Women chefs and head cooks made 76 cents to the dollar men earned in 2019," Narrow the Gap, https://www.narrowthegap.co/gap/chefs-and-head-cooks.

Restaurant Opportunities Centers United, Ending Jim Crow in America's Restaurants: Racial and Gender Occupational Segregation in the Restaurant Industry (New York, NY: ROC United, 2015).

6. Celine McNicholas and Margaret Poydock, "Who are essential workers? A comprehensive look at their wages, demographics, and unionization rates," *Working Economics*, Economics Policy Institute, May 19, 2020, https://www.epi.org/blog/who-are-essential-workers-a-comprehensive-look-at-their-wages-demographics-and-unionization-rates/.

7. Brenda Ann Kenneally, Adrian Nicole LeBlanc, and Tim Arango, "America at Hunger's Edge," *New York Times Magazine*, September 2, 2020, https://www.nytimes.com/interactive/2020/09/02/magazine/food-insecurity-hunger-us.html.

Acknowledgments

I AM PROFOUNDLY grateful to the amazing women who contributed to this book by sharing their talent, time, energy, and words in these pages. I am humbled by your generosity and openness and inspired by your spirit, ingenuity, dedication, and perseverance. Thank you for saying yes.

I'm equally indebted to the women who had conversations with me and who met me for coffee and answered my (many) questions when this idea was just a seedling. Katie Sloan-Palagi, Maryam Ahmed, Jess Thomson, Annie Happel, Lizzie Binder, Christa Chase, Celia Sack, Stevie Stacionis, Sara Forte, Bonnie Tsui, Polina Chesnakova, Leslie Jonath, and Abby Fuller—thank you for meeting this idea with enthusiasm, assistance, and encouragement from the start.

Kate Woodrow, my superhuman agent and friend—thank you for believing in me, sticking with me, and keeping the faith that the right project would, indeed, strike at the right time. You have guided me through every aspect of this process; you bolstered my courage and gave me confidence to keep going. Thank you, thank you, thank you for being my steady cheerleader, my clear-headed coach, my honest and insightful advisor, and my fierce advocate. Also, it has been so. much. fun. I could not have done this without you.

Rachael Mt. Pleasant, my editor—it has been a dream working with you to bring this book to life. Thank you for championing it from the beginning, and for bringing your patience and joy to it. I—and the book—have benefited tremendously from your experienced eye, your unflappable calm, your stellar organization prowess, and your thoughtful and grounded perspective. I am grateful for your ability to consider the tiniest of details and the big picture at once. Thank you for your sage advice and support in honoring my vision, and your thoughtful care in shepherding this book along every step of the way.

Sarah Smith, you approached this puzzle of a book with curiosity and clarity—thank you for bringing it to the page with such balanced and beautiful design. To my team at Workman Publishing—Kate Karol, Barbara Peragine, Julie Primavera, Carol Burrell, Julia Chang, Janet McDonald, Nancy Ringer, Robin Perlow, Jessica Rozler, Rebecca Carlisle, Moira Kerrigan, Kate Oksen, Diana Griffin, Katie Campbell, Hillary Tacuri, and Suzie Bolotin. Thank you for your meticulous attention, integrity, dedication, and flexibility, and for helping me share my book with the world.

To the influential teachers and mentors from whom I've learned multitudes over the years—especially Sherri Ippel, Adele Beckman, Rick Gillett, Will Nash, Deb Evans, Brett Millier, David Bumbeck, Tammy Faulds, Lisa Congdon—you taught me how to think critically and across boundaries, how to work hard and ask questions, how to trust myself and invest in my own creativity. Thank you.

Palma—there is literally no way I would have been able to pull this off without you being part of our family's life. Thank you for dedicating many hours to Lucy and Maggie, for bringing them steadiness and joy (especially through this wild year), for your help transcribing interviews, and for just helping keep our ship afloat.

To the strong and inspiring women who I am lucky to count as dear friends—Sommerville, Kate, Hannah, Bibba, Leah, Chloe, Jenna, and Sara. Thank you for showing up in all the ways, even from afar, for checking in and listening, for sharing your wit, love, and wisdom, and for cheering me on. Going through life with you all is an incredible fortune.

And my family—any dream I've ever had, had a chance because of you. I carry your collective love with me everywhere and always. Thank you, especially to my Grandma Tutu, for your quiet fortitude and courage and for modeling resilience. And Jojo and Bapa, I learned so much sitting at your kitchen table. Thank you for showing me the power of gathering, for reinforcing over and over the meaning of sacrifice and gratitude, for modeling humor, grace, and an abiding faith in something bigger.

Mom and Dad, your unconditional and enduring love, generosity, and support have always been and will always be my constant buoy. You nurtured my creativity even, and especially, in moments when I wanted to give up. You taught me how to rely on myself and my instincts, to have trust and patience in uncertain moments and the unfolding of time, and to find joy and laughter all the while. You

helped me ask hard questions and not shy away from the answers. Thank you for empowering me with confidence and for relentlessly encouraging me to follow my heart and do what I love. Words feel inadequate to express my love and gratitude. Thank you, thank you, to the moon and back.

Lucy and Maggie, your contagious curiosity and optimism are a wellspring of hope. I am grateful for every part of being your mom; you teach me how to keep an open heart, how to look for beauty and magic, and how to absorb each present moment. I will always remember the sweet years working on this book, you two and your wide eyes tumbling into my studio to ask if you could help. You did help—your boundless energy and excitement during the many hours I spent working on it carried me through. I hope it makes you proud. I hope when you hold it in your hands and look through it that you are reminded of the shining promise of your futures, and that now and in the years ahead you believe, as I do, that you can be and do a great many things.

And lastly, Craig—you're at the end because everything returns to you. My partner in it all, your love and confidence in me have held fast since the day we met, and you have been by my side through every peak and valley. Thank you for renewing my faith in myself when I doubted it, for making me laugh and take breaks when I was tired, for supporting me when I felt overwhelmed, and for knowing when I needed space. This life—this adventure with you—is a gift I'll never get over, and I'm eternally grateful. I love you.

About the Author

LINDSAY GARDNER is an illustrator and artist who lives in Oakland, California, with her husband and two daughters (her favorite sous chefs). Her penchant for stories and art led her from her hometown of Grand Rapids, Michigan, to Middlebury College, where she studied American literature and art, and San Francisco Art Institute, where she earned her MFA in painting. Her illustrations have appeared in cookbook and editorial projects, advertising campaigns, and stationery and interior design collaborations, and have been featured on Eatingwell.com and in *Flow* and *Uppercase* magazines, among others. This is her first book.

To see more of her work, visit lindsaygardnerart.com.

BELOW

Gardner's kitchen